Still Rowing on the Snohomish
In the Bounty of the River

Bill Jaquette

ARJ Publishing

Copyright © 2024 by Bill Jaquette

All rights reserved. This book or any portion thereof may not be reproduced or used in any manner whatsoever without the express written permission of the publisher, except for the use of brief quotations in a book review.

ISBN (Paperback): 978-1-7379328-2-6
ISBN (eBook): 978-1-7379328-3-3

Interior Formatting & Cover Design by Aaxel Author Group

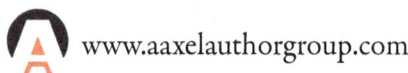 www.aaxelauthorgroup.com

This book is designed for entertainment purposes only. You should not rely on this information as a substitute for, nor does it replace, professional advice related to health and fitness. If you have any concerns or questions about your health, you should always consult with a physician or other health-care professional.

To all my rowing friends who help me stay afloat.

Foreword

I have long known that exercise is one of the keys to health. For many years, I did what many people did: go running. But running for me was always just a task often done in the early-morning darkness, not infrequently in the rain, and sometimes on a path by an angry dog. My distaste often allowed me to find an excuse not to go. I had to find something better for me. I have been involved in boating all my life and knew how to row—rowing a small dinghy within an area of a couple hundred yards to go fishing or to meet up with another boat. However, I had never thought of it as something worthy in itself.

In my early days on the water sailing and fishing, I would see others out rowing in shells and like most people growing up in western Washington, I was well aware of the exploits of the University of Washington crew. But I had not given it a try myself until I entered law school and bought a single shell as a diversion from my studies. That time on the water and away from shore was the start of my progression to a full dedication to rowing, more precisely sculling, as a major part of my way of life.

Along the way, my focus on rowing has led me to build three

wooden boats. The first was a cosine wherry. The book *Rip, Strip & Row*, by J. D. Brown, provided the plans and instructions for construction of a fourteen-foot rowing boat, designed by John Hartsock, that was built out of three-quarter-inch cedar strips. From that success and with the help of a number of boat-building classes, I built a seventeen-foot Whitehall of classic lapstrake construction (like the Viking ships) from a table of offsets I found in *Building Classic Small Craft, Volume 1*, by John Gardner. My pride and joy to this day, I have taken *Thurgood* on a number of rowing/camping trips in the San Juan Island in Washington State and the Gulf Islands in British Columbia, Canada. The third boat, a true rowing shell, I built from plans that I created on a computer boat-design program. While a success in its own way, it was too heavy and was destroyed in my efforts to make it lighter.

Further along the way, I discovered Sound Rowers, an organization that sponsors a number of regattas inviting any human-powered crafts—kayaks, canoes, peddle boats, and rowing boats of all kinds—to race on various open-water courses around western Washington. Over the years, I raced each of those boats that I built, and the sculls I have purchased to succeed them, in many of the Sound Rowers races. However, rowing didn't become the major part of my way of life until I placed my boat in the boathouse of the Everett Rowing Association and started rowing on the Snohomish River.

The Snohomish River is the child of the Skykomish and Snoqualmie Rivers that pass on to the Snohomish the waters they have brought down from the Cascade Mountains. A little further downstream the Pilchuck River adds its mountain waters to the flow. By the time they reach the Snohomish, the raging waters from the mountains have calmed, but there still is a substantial current in the Snohomish that varies with the flow from the mountains. The River empties into Puget Sound and, with its course never far above sea level, the state of the tides will also affect the current often causing it to flow upriver.

Rowing is now the most significant thing I do for exercise. I row an average of three times per week, varying more or fewer based on the weather. Each outing lasts about an hour and a half. Unlike some people who enjoy exercise for its own sake, I need something more to inspire me into action. That is the job of the Snohomish River.

In 2017, I published *Rowing on the Snohomish*. The book consists of four chapters, one for each season of the year. Each chapter contains stories of my rowing on the Snohomish River in that season. They are based primarily on the events of a particular outing, but I have added some events from other outings to give a fuller picture of what I am experiencing.

Each season is different. Winter is the story of struggling with limited daylight, cold, windy, and wet weather, and the occasional rewards for my struggles to get out there. Much of the story of spring is about the revival of the trees and plants and the emergence of the birds and other animals, and the other rowers. Summer is a time for taking some longer expeditions along alternate waterways. On expeditions in the fall, I experience the shortening of the day and the cooling temperatures, the return of the fog, the trees losing their leaves, and the birds settling down for winter or planning to fly south to avoid it. In every season I get to experience the trees along the shore with the mountains rising behind, the sky in all its varieties, and their reflections in the calm waters of the river.

In the seven years since I wrote *Rowing on the Snohomish* things have changed. There has been more global warming and there is a different political party in the Whitehouse, but I am thinking of things closer to home. The pair of bald eagles that used to greet me from Eagle Tree have moved elsewhere. Happily, some of the large derelict vessels that had been left on my river have been removed, to be replaced, unhappily, by several others. However, the biggest change for me is the simple passage of time.

My body is making it clear that I am in my 80s. I'm rowing slower. In 2016, I was averaging over 7 miles an hour when I rowed; in 2020, the average was down to about 6.25 and now it's less than 6. The diminishing cartilage in my back has also made me very cautious about lifting anything heavy over my head. But of most concern to me has been the struggle I have every now and again, particularly when it turns wet, cold, and windy, motivating myself to get on the water.

To ease the concern with my back I have developed procedures using a dolly to get my single scull in and out of the water without having to lift it onto my back. I can get the boat off the rack, wheel it down to the dock and get it into the water, and, upon completing a row, get it out of the water, up the ramp and back on its rack without putting any weight over my head.

To help me with my struggling motivation, I keep harkening back to the doctor congratulating me on the extra back muscles I had developed from rowing, and the realization that once I get on the water and put that body to work, I would find myself in a state of mind that replaced my focus on all those negatives.

I have been keeping a log of all my times on the water since 2010. From my Speed Coach, a device that records the rotations of an impeller attached to the bottom of my boat, I get my speed and distance through the water on each row, and total that up as the year continues. I also write a one-line story about the things I encountered. I have been able to record over 1000 miles every year since then. Continuing in that string has been a good way to keep motivated.

I found an even more powerful motivator when retirement made it no longer necessary to get up in the dark to find time to row. I joined the masters rowers of the Everett Rowing Association and Mill Town Rowing.

Part One of this book presents stories of my experiences over the last seven years and continuing on today. Part Two repeats my stories in *Rowing on the Snohomish*.

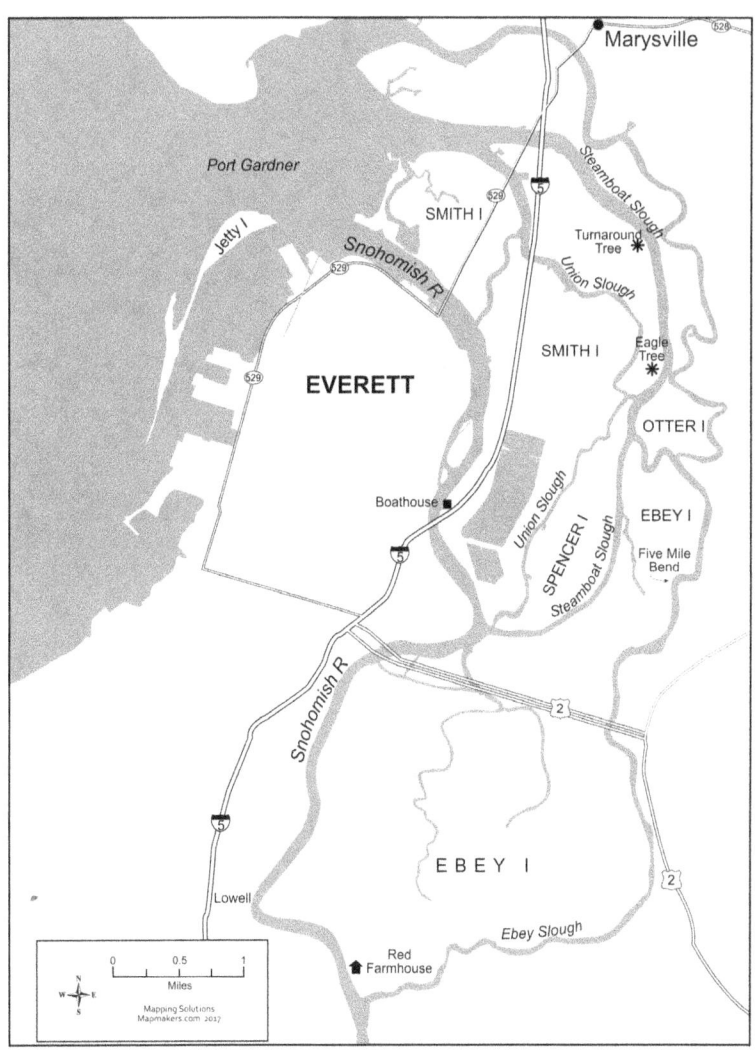

Rowing on the Snohomish Map

Brett's Photo "Mount Rainier, Steamboat Slough, and Me"[1]

---

1 While on the water on his job for Snohomish County Brett Gaddis took this picture of Mount Rainier and me.

Glossary

You rowers will have no troubles with these terms, but I also want people who have never rowed to share my experiences. To that end I offer this glossary of terms that might not be a part of your vocabulary.

Catch a Crab: The oar fails to come out of the water at the release and acts as a brake to the boat.

Dolphin: A group of three, four, sometimes more, pilings tied together at the top standing tall out of the water, used for moorage or for protection of something in the water.

Feathered Oar: Oar blade is rolled over parallel to the water for the recovery.

Rack: The supports in a boathouse on which the rowing shells are stored.

Sling: A device used to temporarily support a shell while it remains on land being prepared to be launched or to be put away.

Skeg: A fin attached to the bottom of a rowing shell that helps to keep it on course.

Spacers: Little plastic devices used to make adjustments to the height of the oarlock.

Stroke: One complete cycle of the catch, drive, release, and recovery.

Catch: The oar blade is put into the water to start the stroke

Drive: Pulling the oar through the water to propel the boat

Release: Lifting the oar out of the water at the end of the drive.

Recovery: Bringing the oar blade forward to begin the next stroke.

Foot Stretcher: Two inclined footrests with shoes that hold the rower's feet.

Oarlock: A device that holds the oar to the boat and becomes the pivot point for the stroke.

Rigger: The device attached to the boat holding the oarlock out away from the hull giving the oar greater leverage in the drive.

Sliding Seat: A seat that slides up and back that enables the rower to use their legs to enhance the drive.

Speed Coach: A device that measures the rotation of an impeller attached to the bottom of the boat and measures the speed and distance traveled through the water, the number of strokes per minute, and the length of time rowing.

PART 1

ONE

I've Got a Lot to Learn

Day One

With the additional time on my hands retirement provided, I decided to sign up to join one of the masters rowing sessions sponsored by the Everett Rowing Association. I had been storing my shells in the Association's boathouse to facilitate a quick launch, but with all my time at work it was easier to schedule my own solo time on the water. I had seen the club masters and juniors on the water, and I will confess that what they were doing looked a lot easier than what I'd been doing. Their sessions were shorter than mine and they were sharing their efforts with other rowers in the same boat. So, when I showed up for a masters session, I was pretty confident.

I got assigned to a Quad and would be rowing for the first time ever with three other people. A Quad is much heavier than my Single and it took a team effort to lift it off its rack in the boathouse, carry it outside, flip it right side up, and set it down on a pair of slings. There my fellow crew members busied themselves making adjustments to the foot-stretchers to accommodate their height, and to choose the number of spacers under their oarlocks so the blade of the oar would travel through the water at the right depth. I was lost. I hadn't made any of those changes in my boats since I bought them. Thankfully, another member of our crew helped determine the right adjustments for me. There were already things I needed to learn.

But it was time to launch. As always when more than one person is involved in a project somebody is in charge. For us that was the Bow, the rower assigned to seat one. On her command, the four of us swung the boat upside down over our heads and down on our shoulders, then carried it down the ramp to the dock. Once there we moved over to the edge, swung the boat over our heads and down into the water. This was truly a coordinated effort that we needed to get right every time to avoid damaging the boat or hurting someone. We then put in the oars, climbed in on the command "one foot in and down," got ourselves situated, and shoved away.

I was ready to row, but apparently the Bow was still in charge, and she had other instructions. The stern pair (seats three and four) was told to row: "arms and body only, square blade." Luckily, I was in seat two and could learn by watching. That command required the rower to keep their legs straight, not using the sliding seat, and to row with the oar blades perpendicular to the surface of the water. It soon went to "half slide," then "full slide" still with square blades. So far, I'd made no mistakes, but then I'd just sat there with my oars dragging through the water. I was paying close attention to what the stern pair was doing because I would certainly be called to perform the same routine any moment. After the stern pair had rowed about 20 strokes following each of those commands, the Bow called out "way-nuff" and the stern pair stopped rowing. I immediately added that phrase to my mental dictionary, later learning "way-nuff" was short for "way enough," which as I had guessed meant stop rowing. It was now my turn, together with the Bow. The "arms and body," "half slide," and "full slide" were simple enough, but not the "square blade." I kept catching my blade on the water, interrupting my stroke, and splashing water back at the boat. I was ready to be done with this, and after the Bow and I completed the exercises, we also got to "way-nuff."

We were now going to row together and, for the first time in my life, I was going to have to stay in sync with other rowers. That wasn't as simple as I had imagined it. I kept falling behind the rhythm of the other rowers, leaving my oar in the water to be struck by the blade of the rower in seat three, or get ahead of the others and strike the blade of the rower in seat one. The other rowers were very understanding, but I was embarrassed. We rowed along for a while, and I would have periods when I could get myself into the proper rhythm but, about the time I started thinking that I was getting the hang of it I would strike another oar.

Despite my fumbling, we were able to make substantial progress up the River to the Highway 2 Bridge. To keep the boat on course the bow seat would occasionally order us to pull more on starboard or on port. I knew what "starboard" and "port" meant from my sailing days, but facing backwards port was now on my right side and starboard on my left, and it would take me just a little longer to get it right. These were things I had never had to consider. Pulling left and pulling right to adjust the course in my Single shell was often done below the level of the conscious mind and "port" and "starboard" were never part of the consideration.

At the Bridge we turned around. On the Bow's command, we pulled forward with our starboard oar and pushed backwards with the port, again and again, and the boat gradually turned around and came to rest. Then again on the Bow's calls "Ready all, Ready, Row" we started rowing and headed back to the dock. It was the middle of the ebb tide which added to the speed of the river's current, and we moved swiftly down river toward the dock. The considerable amount of water moving along the river created eddies that would force the boat to pull to one side then the other requiring a constant chain of commands for adjustment from the Bow. To be able to land against the current, we rowed past the dock, turned the boat around again, and came in for a landing.

We derigged the oars, then the four of us leaned out over the boat and, on command, swung it bottom up over our heads. With the water we had splashed in while rowing—mostly from me—draining out over us, we lowered the boat down to our shoulder, walked it up the ramp and set it down in its slings. After a quick wash, rinse, and dry, the boat was put away, stories were exchanged, and we all went home.

I had been treated with nothing but kindness, but I still can remember going home that day feeling in despair. I'd been sculling for 40 years and should be able set my stroke at the same rate as the others. I considered dropping out of the group rowing. I could still come down to the river and launch my Single shell and enjoy all the other pleasures of rowing on the Snohomish. But that would be letting my ego control. With a little more humility in my heart, I should be able to go out on a team boat again with the realization that I still had things to learn.

Out in a Quad

Day Two

I spent not a little time at home wondering what I should do now. I had learned everything I knew about rowing on my own, rowing around Mercer Island in Lake Washington, joining in Sound Rowers races around Shaw Island in the San Juan Islands and across Puget Sound and back in the shadow of the City of Seattle, and solo rowing in the San Juans and Canada. Maybe I just learned to do it wrong. Although my doubts didn't leave me, that ego that had been punishing me for not being a better rower commanded me to try again.

I was again placed in seat two in a Quad, and our launch went smoothly. I had at least learned my part in that process. This time we headed down river against the upriver current of a flooding tide. My mission for the day was to match my stroke with the other rowers. I tried to copy exactly the movements of the rower in front of me (seat three) as she pushed her oar handles out in front of her; leaned forward; pulled herself ahead on the sliding seat; then dropped her oar blades into the water for the drive. As long as I stayed fully focused things seemed to go ok, but, when my mind wandered even little bit, there was a good chance of another clash of oars. I came to realize that copying the rower in front of me wasn't going to be enough to fit me into the team. My three fellow rowers were controlling their stroke from their feel for the rhythm of the boat. That is something I was going to have to find, hopefully, with more time on the water.

There were other shells on the river, another Quad like ours, a couple of Doubles, and one Eight, and we needed to be sure that we didn't find ourselves on a collision course with any of them. If I had been rowing my Single, that would be my responsibility; in our Quad that was the responsibility of the Bow seat and she had us moving to port or starboard as needed to stay clear of the others.

As we rowed past Dagmar's Landing, a large power cruiser cast off its lines and sped down the river past our fleet of rowers. It managed to avoid hitting anyone but did set up a large wake and we all stopped rowing as the series of its waves sent us up and down, up and down; rolling over to one side then the other, again and again and again. Fortunately, although several of us shipped a little water, we all stayed upright, the waves passed, and we began to row again. A few minutes later another cruiser pulled out of Dagmar's and moved at a no-wake speed past our fleet to "thank-yous" from several of the rowers.

The day was getting warmer and as we paused to rest, I watched several of the rowers take off a layer. With one hand holding the oars, the other hand grabbed the collar and pulled the coat over their head into their lap. The sleeves were then removed and the coat stashed away. Simple enough, but I had always removed a layer by reaching behind my back with both arms to pull the sleeves off first. And every time, I imagined my oars getting loose and the boat capsizing with me unable to swim because my arms were caught behind my back. What everybody out here rowing knew, was a revelation to me that has made me safer ever since.

From there all the boats rowed under the Hwy 529 Bridge and the railroad bridge that paralleled it, heading toward Port Gardner Bay. A train of cars filled with coal was crossing the bridge as we passed below, and we were serenaded by the banging and screeching as it rolled over us.

Down here beyond the bridge we saw a number of harbor seals pop their heads out of the water and give us a look. A little further along we rowed by a series of pilings standing over ten feet out of the water, on which cormorants, seagulls, and an eagle were perched. On one an osprey stood guard on its nest of sticks.

We had almost made it to Jetty Island, but it was time to head back. On the Bow's command, we turned the boat around and started rowing upriver. I still had a lot to learn about rowing with others and several times on the way back I took a bad stroke out of sync with the others. On one occasion I made my recovery too fast and caught the bow seat's starboard oar at the end of her stroke. But that was my only major mistake, and there were times when I found myself rowing to the rhythm of the boat. With still plenty to learn, I was going to become a team rower.

Day Three

Any time a group of Everett Rowers gets on the water there is a coach alongside driving an aluminum outboard boat—we call it a launch.

Their first responsibility is the safety of the rowers, followed by the safety of the equipment. They are also highly trained rowers who can offer suggestions to individual rowers and exercises to the whole group to help them improve. Their first duty of the day, however, is to decide which boats to take out, which rowers will be assigned to which boats and at which seats. For this outing, in addition to the two Quads and one Double, there were going to be three of us in Single shells. Although I had learned a lot about team rowing, it was a bit of relief to be rowing in a boat by myself.

The three of us were the first on the water and we rowed a short distance while the Double and Quads launched. The coach motored out and told us to row upriver through the I-5 Bridge, but then wait for the others because we were going to do some drills.

When we had all arrived together, the coach motored up and told us to start the dribble drill (also known as the dip-dip drill) at the release. I knew what the release position was, but not the dribble part. Looking around I saw the other rowers sitting in their boats at ease holding the blades of their oars perpendicular to the water dipping them in and out of the water. Well, that was simple enough and I joined in, but I couldn't see how that was going to make me a better rower. The coach's next call was to do the same thing at half slide. I found it a little harder, but I could do it. The coach's third call was for the same thing at full slide and now I was having a hard time keeping the boat balanced. If nothing else the drill showed me my rowing skills could be improved. The next drill had us row one full stroke followed by a pause at the hands away position; then another full stroke followed by a pause at hands away and the body forward. This procedure was repeated with pauses at half slide and then full slide. This went pretty well for me once I got the order into my head. When we completed our drills, it was time to just go rowing. I went home that night questioning the value of these drills, but as time went on, with these drills a regular feature of the group outings, I came to accept they were part of the art of sculling.

As we started rowing upriver the coach motored over alongside and watched me row, then asked me to stop. He complemented my rowing style but said I needed to keep the oars fully out of the water on the recovery. I had gotten into the bad habit of dragging my oars across the water for the pleasant sound of their rattle through the wavelets. He also suggested that I slow the last part of my slide in the recovery, explaining it would avoid driving the stern down deeper into the water and slowing the boat. In the days that followed I received a number of critical suggestions from coaches and other rowers. I had been rowing for years collapsing the movement of the arms, body, and sliding the seat into a single maneuver, but learned to hold off sliding the seat aft until first pushing the oars handles forward and leaning the body forward, then sliding the seat aft to the catch position. I also learned that I could take a longer stroke by making placement of the oar into the water not part of the drive but part of the recovery, and by leaning further back before ending it. There was no question that these suggestions were making me a better rower.

We had a good row up the river but turned around in front of the Newland Construction Company business shortly after passing under the Hwy 2 bridge and rowed home.

Don't Stop Now

The Eight

When I arrived at the boathouse, the other rowers were collected around the boat assignment board where we were to learn what boat we were to row. Uh-oh, there were only going to be two boats, both Eights and I was assigned to row seat three in the *Engel*. My skill level had improved in rowing in boats with others, but we had always been sculling, rowing with an oar in each hand, an art I had been practicing on my own for 40 years. In an Eight I would be rowing with both hands, on one much longer oar. I had known this was going to happen eventually but wasn't really ready for this to be the day.

Both boats were going to be mixed, rowed by teams of both women and men. The team in the other boat was younger on average and more experienced than our team and they would be training to row in some regattas scheduled during the year. I had rowed in boats with most of the rowers on our team and, although not high performers, they still knew their stuff and we were going to have some fun on the water.

I had made note of the coordinated effort it took for the four rowers to manage a Quad on shore and getting it to and from the water. Now an Eight is half again as heavy and half again as long as a Quad and requires the coordinated efforts of all eight rowers under the command of the Coxswain (Cox) to launch. Once again as the novice on the team I was often corrected as to my part in the task, but we were able to safely launch the *Engel* and climb in ready to row.

Sitting in seat three in anticipation of what was about to happen I was thinking how different sweep rowing was going to be. The basic mechanics couldn't be much different than sculling and I had often watched sweep rowing over the years. However, I was sitting there for the first time holding onto something that was three feet longer than the device I was accustomed to, and I was going to have to operate it in perfect coordination with seven other rowers who knew what they were doing.

I knew that the boat was equipped with a cox box with speakers located at several places along the boat but had not experienced one in operation until sitting there with my oar resting on the water, I heard the hollow sound of a quick test breath of air over the speaker followed by a command to "shove off." We all pushed away and were soon free of the dock. The bow pair rowed us out into the middle of the river where, hearing "way- nuff," they stopped, and we all sat at ease with our oars skimming across the water and the boat slowing to a stop. The call came out "stern six, sitting ready" and I realized that my time of anticipation had come to an end. "Arms and body, row," came the command and we were off. The boat was moving slowly, and by paying careful attention to the rowers in the seats in front of me, I was able to match their body movements. "Arms and body" became "half slide" then "full slide" and we rowed at full stroke for about a minute. On the command "three and four out, bow pair in" the whole drill was repeated, but this time without me, and I had a few moments to be at ease. On the command "five and six out, three and four in" I was back at it, and I continued rowing during the final stage of this drill with the "stern pair out, five and six in."

It was now time to do some "steady state" rowing at 50% maximum effort and what had seemed like something I could do showed itself to be a much greater challenge. We were rowing much faster at a higher stroke rate and time and again I would pull the oar out of the water before the end of the drive and occasionally fail completely to get the blade into the water.

As we continued along, I focused on keeping my oar in the water during the drive and was managing to reduce these mistakes when, failing to get my blade out of the water in time, I suddenly got hit in the chest with the handle of my oar. Every rower knows what it means to catch a crab. I had caught a few little 'sand crabs' over the years rowing my Single which I easily handled. But an Eight moves through the water faster and with more force and the longer oar gives the crab much more power. The oar handle can end up behind the rower and occasionally throw the rower out of the boat. This time I just took a hit in the chest, but that experience was one more lesson for me about rowing in an Eight.

We were rowing at ease but moving faster than I had ever rowed. The Cox was able to steer the boat with the rudder, but as we neared a bend in the river I heard "starboard pressure, port lighter." The other starboard rowers and I pulled harder with the port rowers easing up, and the boat moved smoothly around the point.

Just before Highway 2 we turned the boat around, pulling forward on port, pushing back on starboard. Once on our line we began to row again and were soon back at the dock and done for the day.

Rowing in an Eight

Singles

When the covid epidemic arrived a number of our rowers, along with many other rowers across the country, became leery about rowing in team boats. My concern increased when I learned about the forty members of a nearby community choir getting sick after singing together at their practice. I could see a real parallel to rowing in a team boat with rowers sitting four feet apart and breathing hard. Many people stopped rowing, some not to be seen on the water again. Some found the solution by starting to row in Singles, leaving the Eights, Quads, and Doubles on their racks in the boathouse.

This morning six of us were going to be on the water, all in Singles. I was comfortable because I'd been rowing Singles all my rowing life, but three of the group had very little experience in a Single. At our prelaunch assembly one of the rowers, Kathy, announced this was going to be her first time in a Single but seemed relieved by the encouragement from the other rowers and the promise from the coach that he would keep a close eye on her.

There are different kinds of Single sculls: the racing scull is 27 feet long, slim, and very tippy, designed for rowing fast on smooth water. Two of the group and I were in racing shells. There are other shell designs, between 20 and 25 feet, designed to row in open water where it is frequently rougher. Our three novice companions were rowing in these open water shells. I have an open water shell of my own that I like to row during the winter months because its greater stability is good to have when the water is colder, and the winds can be strong.

There was a light fog that promised to clear, and glassy smooth water. We headed upriver and into Steamboat Slough. The three racing shells moved out ahead but paused at the mouth of the Slough to wait for the others to catch up. Watching them approach, we could tell they knew how to row, but the limited stability of a Single was causing them trouble.

Singles in the Fog

When we had all collected together, the coach pulled up and told us all to head down Steamboat but gather up again at the entrance to Ebey Slough. Again, the three racing shells moved out ahead, with me the distance third. Upon reaching Ebey we spun around and waited for the others. When the last three rowers pulled up, Kathy moved over toward me. Still nervous about the instability of rowing a Single, she was nevertheless enjoying being completely in command and I congratulated her for managing to stay afloat and row this far. But as if that were a cue for the devil, as she pulled away, Kathy's starboard oar swung high out of the water, her port oar blade diving deep into the water. Desperately trying to stay upright she leaned to starboard and tried to get both oars back onto the surface of the water, but it was too late. She had already tipped too far and was soon in the water with her arms slung over her capsized boat.

The center of buoyance is the location on any boat where the volume of the hull below that point displaces enough water to keep the boat afloat. The center of gravity is the center of the mass of the boat and everything in it. To keep them stable, sail and power boats are designed with the center of gravity below the center of buoyancy. With a rower sitting in a shell, that center of gravity is far above the center of buoyancy at about the rower's beltline, making stability the primary challenge of rowing. Kathy paid the penalty when she allowed her shell to tip too far to port and her center of gravity to pull her over.

The coach was quickly by her side and pulled her aboard the launch to the applause of the other rowers. Kathy could have chosen to be carried back to the dock in the launch, but decided instead to get back in the shell, once it was righted and bailed, and continue to row. We all made it back to the dock without further incident. While putting things away those of us who had managed to stay dry on this day went over to Kathy to confess our own trips into the water.

THREE

A True Story

Most of what I write is officially fiction. It reflects my experiences and observations, but I can't claim things happened just the way I describe them. This is a true story.

I love rowing on the water and having friends out there with me makes it even more fun. However, rowing in an Eight is not my favorite way to do it. I know it's not fair but sitting there on an Eight with a crew of rowers pulling hard in front and behind me, brings to mind Charlton Heston in *Ben Hur* rowing that war galley into battle. Coordinating the efforts of eight rowers requires an unquestioned obedience not necessary in a Single. But that was the order of the day, and it was going to be great to be together on the water with a crew of friends. However, I didn't know at the time, but I was going to find myself undergoing something even closer to the experience Heston portrayed.

It was March 5th, 2022, and the promise of spring was in the air. Two masters Eights were to be launched. One was to be powered by the club's women rowers trying to gear themselves up to race in the Opening Day Regatta in Seattle and other venues thereafter. In 2022, there weren't enough men in the club to fill a competitive Eight so the other Eight, the *Engel*, was to be powered by rowers at an assortment of skill levels. Our Stroke in seat eight was Aaron Haack, probably the club's strongest rower. He would be setting the stroke rate that we all had to follow. Brett Parks was in seat seven, responsible for balancing the power of the Stroke. Seats six, five, four, and three are considered the engine room of a shell responsible for producing the power of the boat. Bob Alo was in seat six, a guest rower John Vignos, in five, Eric Schwager in four, and Andy Egloff in three. That left the bow pair, Carolyn Thostenson in seat one and me in seat two. We borrowed a junior rower Aidan Richer to be our Cox.

Both Eights were launched, and we headed out in the company of coach Drew McCrea who had Ramon Wallace, a masters rower beached with an injury, along as a guest. The Snohomish is a tidal river, and we were out during an ebb tide where the lowering water level in Port Gardner Bay was inviting the river to increase the speed of its current. Our progress upriver was slowed but with a promise for a speedy return. The two Eights stayed close together rowing at a steady state, focusing on coordinating the energies of the rowers. My sweep rowing skills had improved, but there were still several times when my oar blade would come out of the water before the end of the drive.

Somewhere upriver from the Highway 2 Bridge we turned around and headed back to the dock in the rapidly flowing river. Although nothing was said, it felt to me that a competitive feeling between the two boats materialized and got stronger as we passed the entrance to Steamboat Slough and were headed back to the dock. As I recall we were a little ahead of the women's boat approaching the I-5 bridge when one of its women yelled a warning that there was a log in our path. Sitting so low in the water that it was difficult to see was a long slender log that was indeed in our path and before anything could be done, I felt the log bump its way along the bottom and our boat come to a stop.

We were not moving through the water, but the water was still on the move, and it swung the boat around perpendicular to the flow, aimed right at the one of the huge cement piers of the I-5 bridge. It was soon clear we were going to hit the pier and were helpless to prevent it. As we approached, Andy tried to hold the boat off with his oar but on contact his rigger shattered and the boat slammed against the pier and immediately capsized.

The boat was sinking, and I could hear the hull crumbling. I had to get out. My feet were still held in the rowing shoes, and it took some effort to get loose. Pushing away from the boat, I sank headfirst down into the water, and had to twist my body around to get my head pointed up. At the surface I found myself drifting away in the current. Carolyn and Andy had freed themselves too but managed to hang onto the boat. I couldn't see what was happening in the back half of the boat because by this time the current had bent the boat around the pier with those aboard the back half out of my sight.

I thought about swimming to shore. It wasn't too far, but the current was moving fast and the water was really cold. Fortunately, I didn't have to entertain that thought for long because Drew and Ramon motored up and placed a boarding ladder over the side of their launch. I was cold and soaking wet and was struggling to climb up. Ramon leaned over the side to help me but in doing so tipped the boat over so far that it was making my escape harder. When he moved back to the other side, I was able to get my head and shoulders over the gunnel but needed Drew's help to get the rest of my body aboard. Seeing Carolyn and Andy still clinging to the boat, Drew decided to drop me ashore in the care of people there, then race back to the wreck to continue the rescue.

Scott Holmgren was coaching other boats that were rowing behind the speedier Eights. When he noticed the *Engel* sitting at right angles to the current and not moving through the water, he realized that something was wrong and drove his launch at top speed down the river to investigate. By the time he arrived the collision had already occurred. He first helped to free Eric who was stuck in the boat dangerously close to its point of contact with the pier, then got John, Bob, Brett, Aaron, and Aiden on board the launch and took them ashore.

Carolyn had been able to hang on to the capsized boat for a while but in time lost her hold and started to float away. With her heavy winter rowing clothes fully soaked, she sank deep into the water afraid she was going to drown. On his return to the scene, Scott got her aboard the launch and took her ashore. Andy had hung on to the capsized shell the longest and was still there, when, after rescuing me, Drew and Romon came back and brought him ashore.

Once on shore I was escorted up to the boathouse and into the office with the space heaters on high. Carolyn joined me after her rescue and we spent the next while raising our body temperatures out of the hypothermic zone. When it felt safe, wearing a pair of dry pants loaned me by Romon I went home and sat in front of a space heater for the rest of the day. But I was on the water rowing the next day for Singles Sunday. And so were Aaron, Andy, Bob, and Carolyn.

The *Engel* remained wrapped around the pier while all its human cargo was made safe. When the coaches went back out to examine the wreckage, they found the boat completely broken in two. It was still held to the pier by the wire linking the cox box in the stern to the speakers located along the hull. Eventually the crew brought the two pieces ashore and confirmed what everybody had known from the first moment of contact with the pier. The *Engel* had been destroyed.

Crash of the Eight

The Capsize

May 23rd wasn't the best day for rowing, it was cloudy, there was a strong current, and there was some wind, but what happened wasn't the day's fault, it was mine. The Sunday outing for the Everett Rowing Association singles had been cancelled and I was behind on the miles I needed to rowed to reach my thousand for the year. So that Monday morning I packed up and headed to the boathouse for a row by myself. This is something I do all the time. I feel safe on the Snohomish River. I've been rowing there several times a week for almost 20 years and in all my pervious solo trips I had managed to arrive back at the dock upright. I had capsized five times on the river, but each time I either righted the boat and pulled myself back aboard or pushed the boat to the shore and climbed back onboard. This day was going to be different.

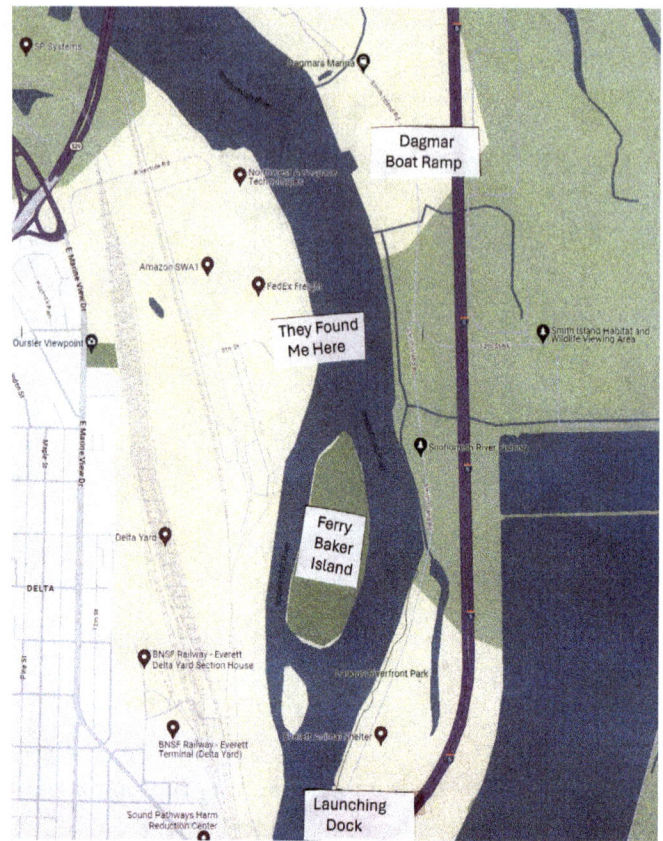

Map of the River, Where it Happened

It was one of those days where I arrived at the boathouse with a part of me looking for an excuse to turn around and go home. As I said, it wasn't the nicest day, and most importantly, I wasn't going to get to be on the water rowing with my friends. But I persevered, loaded *Molly* with all the gadgets and gear and rolled her down to the dock.

The launch went smoothly, and I took off rowing. I headed down river, but within a few strokes I could see that the current was very strong and decided it would be better to go upriver and into Steamboat Slough and down to Otter Island where there would be less current. But when I pulled hard on my starboard oar to make the turn it jumped out of the oarlock. There was mistake number one, I had failed to tighten down the latch that holds the oar into the oarlock. Those of you who row know that scullers depend on the stabilizing effect of the two oars to keep these very narrow hulls upright. With one of those stabilizers gone, I fell over the side into the 40-something degree water and *Molly* rolled over bottom up.

As I said, I'd been here before. My last solo rollover occurred several years before in Steamboat Slough in February. I had righted the boat on that occasion, climbed in, rowed back to the dock, went home, and took a long hot shower. This time, with the oar out of its oarlock, I thought it would be easier to swim the boat to shore where I could lock the oar back in place and row back to the dock. Ferry Baker Island lay directly west of where I was, and the shallows surrounding it made it a perfect place for that maneuver. With *Molly* under one arm, I kicked and paddled with my free arm toward the Island. Mistake number two.

The Bulkhead

The current had a different idea and it swept me down river so that by the time I made it to shore there was no shore, but rather a bulkhead that rose ten feet above the water, where it was too deep for me to touch bottom. There was going to be no way to get out. The current kept pushing me along the bulkhead, but I finally drifted over a horizontal beam on which I could stand and get the upper half of my body out of the water.

I was getting cold and could think of no way to self-rescue my way out of the situation. When I go solo rowing, I carry my cellphone in a waterproof container that I attach to the boat on a 30-inch lanyard. I have used that setup several times to report oil spills on the river and once to announce to a friend that I had just rowed 1000 miles that year. I needed it now to get some help. I held the phone in one hand and punched in 991. No that's not right—hypothermia must be setting in. I punched in 911, but now the phone wasn't working. Mistake number three.

When I purchased my current cellphone, I added a shockproof cellphone case for its protection and a plastic waterproof bag to keep the phone dry and to connect it to that 30-inch lanyard. Together the case and the bag were making it harder for my cold fingers to tap in the numbers I needed. If I was going to make this call, I needed to remove the phone from the waterproof bag—yes, the one with the lanyard that prevents it from falling overboard and down to the bottom of the river—hold it firmly in my hand and make the call. With it clear in my mind that if I dropped the phone into the water, I would lose my best chance for a rescue, I made the call and was greatly relieved to hear: "911 What's your emergency?"

I told the operator my situation and my best guess where I was, and the Everett Police and Fire Departments were deployed to find me. I never saw it, but apparently, they sent up a drone to help them look for me. The police boat had been dispatched but had to turn back because it couldn't get under the railroad bridge. I sat on the beam feeling very cold, talking with the 911 operator hoping someone would hurry up and find me.

In real time it wasn't long before I saw an Everett Police Officer peer over the edge of the bulkhead, and I knew things would start getting better. A ladder was put over the side of the bulkhead, but I didn't want to let go of *Molly* and a better solution soon arrived. The Everett Fire

Department had parked their ambulance on the other side of the river at Dagmar's boat ramp where they launched a rescue boat. The firefighters motored across the river and with a lot of their help I managed to climb aboard for a trip back across to the waiting ambulance.

I was significantly hypothermic, so I was taken to the Providence Hospital Emergency Room where I spent the next several hours wrapped in a blanket with hot air pumped in to bring my body temperature back up to a normal range. As I lay there reliving my adventure, I realized that I'd let go of *Molly* and had visions of her drifting out to Port Gardner Bay, but it turned out that the officers had rescued her too and I was able to retriever her in perfect shape a couple of days later.

Everyone who helped me, the 911 operator, that first Everett Police officer who found me and the fellow officers who arrived to help, the Everett Fire Department crew that shuttled me across the river, into the ambulance and off to the hospital, and the Providence Hospital staff that checked me out and got my body temperature up to normal, everyone did their duties with skill and kindness. *Molly* and I thank them all.

As prescribed, I stayed inactive for the next few days, but by the following weekend I had to go rowing again. I wanted to catch up to the rate of miles rowed that would get me to 1000 for the year, but, more important for me, I needed to rebuild my confidence that a man now 80 can safely enjoy the sport of rowing. Mother Nature must have known what I was thinking because she served up the best weekend for rowing so far this year. The air was warm, the river current minimal, and the water surface glassy smooth. I saw eagles and heron fly overhead; on two occasions harbor seals popped up in my wake, and I got my first sighting of the Canada geese swimming along with their new babies. I was so happy to be back in the game.

FIVE

Derelicts

The one thing that has frustrated me most in all my time rowing on the Snohomish River are the derelicts I keep encountering. I understand that a boat might become too old to serve its purpose, or it might be the boat's owner that gets too old to enjoy using it. And our society doesn't offer the means to easily get rid of an unwanted vessel as it does, say for an unwanted car. But at least for me, considering all the things they have helped humans accomplish over the centuries, boats deserve to be treated with a higher regard than trash, even if they have lost their usefulness. And what is probably more important, the shores of our waterways don't deserve to become the final resting place for abandoned vessels. In centuries past an abandoned boat might well take care of itself when its wooden structure rots away. There is a decaying old wooden barge in the Slough home to bushes and river grass that is well along that path. But today's boats are made out of steel, aluminum, and fiberglass, leaving derelicts around for many human lifetimes.

~

As I imagine it, that old boat has been sitting on its trailer on the side yard unused for a year or two and the outboard engine was hard to start the last time it was out. The family that owns it wants to put a garden on the side yard and their friendly neighbor has assured them that no one would ever want to buy "that thing." Late at night the boat is brought to some lonely spot on the river and sent off to fend for itself. In my trips through the Snohomish River estuary I have encountered a number of such instances of runabout homicide. Removal of these smaller derelicts is fairly simple, but it does cost public tax money to deal with somebody's individual responsibility.

Get this Thing Out of Our Yard

Most of my derelict stories start at what I have come to call the "hospice docks," a series of docks along the south side of waterway, a short ways inside Steamboat Slough. Once there, boats rarely move and every now and then one of them will sink and lay untouched for weeks or months until the Washington Department of Natural Resources (DNR) removes it.

Some years ago now, a very large cruising boat found space on that "hospice docks." When I was rowing by one day, a man at work aboard told me about his plans. The boat had suffered a serious fire and this man had bought it for little or nothing with the intent of repairing it to become something he could enjoy with pride. Over the next year or so, I would see him working on the boat and progress was being made. However there came a time when I was seeing very little activity aboard, the progress slowed even more, and then stopped.

One day I rowed by the dock and found the boat no longer there. It had been moved about a mile down the Slough and anchored in the entrance to the Spencer Island Swamp where it spent a number of months. There were still people on board and they assured me on several occasions that the boat was going to be moved. One day, however, I could see that it had been abandoned. But it remained anchored with a stern tie to the shore and would go aground whenever the water was low. It remained on the Slough deteriorating for a number of months until finally hauled away by the DNR at considerable public expense, putting to an end a dream which turned out not to have the energy or the finances to make it happen.

A Dream Comes False

Sometime later a boat named *Midas* found her way onto the "hospice dock." The vessel, called a crane barge had a large barge shaped steel hull with all kinds of machinery aboard dominated by a system of cranes. She didn't stay long and also found her way down the Slough, anchoring in one place and then another. No one lived aboard, but the vessel was frequently visited by a small outboard motorboat and I often saw one or two people working aboard. I spoke to one of the crew on a couple of occasions and was assured that they had plans to remove *Midas* from the Slough. It moved from one location to another up the Slough and was finally left tied up to some of the dolphins out on the River.

Her crew never showed up again and she sat there until we became a little afraid she would become a permanent part of the river scenery. The DNR finally took control of *Midas* and moved her to a different location further upriver across from the Everett riverfront. But there it stayed and stayed some more until the DNR found the $250,000 it took to chop it up and haul it away.

Midas

That row of dolphins on the River became a popular place to abandon a vessel. Next to arrive was a sailboat remaining there unattended for a number of months, finally sinking with its mast sticking out into the river as a minor hazard to us stern facing rowers. After the sailboat was removed, a houseboat moved in, but it started out occupied and there was a small outboard motorboat which took one of the two occupants off to work each day. That didn't last long, however. The outboard motorboat disappeared, and the house remained unoccupied and eventually it too was removed. In an attempt to deter further visits the City of Everett posted no-trespassing signs on the dolphins in that part of the river. I am not sure what effect such sighs would have had on the three visitors, but no boats have moved in since.

Out rowing one day I saw a houseboat that had been moored inside an inlet off Steamboat Slough now sitting unmoored at the mouth of the inlet. On my next row, I encountered it sitting midstream in the Slough. Over my next few outings I found it at the mouth of Spencer Island Swamp, then partway into the Swamp then far into the swamp where it sits today. I never saw anybody aboard, but as variable as are the currents in the Slough can be, it would be very hard to believe that someone wasn't working hard to dispose of another vessel that had outlived its value.

Houseboat Adrift

I am going to try to remain polite and say I am just frustrated. All of the stories so far end with someone without the resources to deal with a responsibility they accepted when they took on a project that they were hoping would bring them something worthwhile. I don't claim to have all the facts, but this is my read from what we all can see.

The *O&M-1* has been beached along the shore of Steamboat Slough for a long time. Of more recent construction than the *Midas,* she has a much larger crane that is fully rotating. When it first arrived I thought she was being moored temporarily. It had the proud name of a large company that was and remains involved in major marine construction projects up and down the west coast, and I kept believing she was going to move out at any time to a new work assignment. But she never did and continues to sit there on the beach with the high water topping off the water that fills her hull only to drain out part way at low water.

If anyone in this story had the resources to easily remove their derelict from the shores of our River it would have been, and still is this marine construction company.

The O&M—1

Canada Geese

We have been enjoying seeing the new baby Canada geese on the river. During March, April, and May the mother goose lays one egg every day and a half, then sits on the nest to incubate the clutch for 28 days, when on average five to seven, but as many as ten babies would be born. The population of Canada geese has been growing along the river in recent years. All the human activity in the area is one of the reasons for the increase. The resulting reduction in the number of coyotes and other predators has allowed the geese to flourish. It had been fun to watch the baby goslings swimming along the shore in line behind their parents or gathered together on shore.

But the time had come to get serious. It happen every year when the tiny babies grow a little bigger. Their moms and dads bring them up on our launching dock to continue their lessons on what it means to be a goose. Apparently, the rules of personal hygiene are pretty loose for a goose and the first rowers of the day will find themselves greeted by a dock covered with goose poop.

Seems Harmless Enough

In my days rowing alone, I would often be that first person on the water and would clean off a small piece of the dock, just enough to get launched. When the club rowers arrived, however, it became necessary to clean the whole dock and a contingent of "volunteers" would sweep the material into the water with brooms and scrapers then splash the deck clean with buckets of water pulled from the river. When I got more active in the club's group rowing activities, I too helped sweep and splash the dock clean. But *Genesis* tells us that man was given dominion over "every living thing that moves on the earth," and "over the birds of the heavens."[2] But in no way was it dominion, having to scrub our dock every time we wanted to go rowing. Something had to be done.

The geese were using the cover of darkness to make their claim on the dock, so a light source might cause them to get together somewhere else. There was no electricity on the dock so I needed to find a different light source. Inventiveness is one of the sources of man's dominion and I thought that I had found something that might help. Made in China of course, Solar Outdoor Motion Sensor Lights generated their power in their own solar panel and turned the light on with a motion detector. I attached one of these to each of the four metal pilings, so that the

---

2 Genesis 1:26

motion of a goose jumping up on the dock and walking around would turn on the light and scare it back into the water.

I was the first one down to the dock the next morning to see what had happened. There were some small areas on the dock that hadn't been protected, but it looked like we had made some progress. Things looked good the next day too. However, the third morning showed no improvement and by the end of the week all our progress had vanished and the whole dock was covered again with goose poop. The geese had learned there were no further consequences when the lights went on and after they settled down the lights would go off. There were also some portions of the dock that weren't exposed to the motion sensors where the geese could climb onto the dock without being detected at all. Our "dominion over the birds of the heavens" was in jeopardy.

Resolved not to let *Genesis* down, I went back to the source of all human knowledge, Amazon, and found the Solar Outdoor Motion Sensor Alarm. Also made in China, this solar powered motion detector set off a bright flashing red light and a loud pulsating alarm. Those geese weren't going to sit around with this going on. In analyzing my prior failure, it hand occurred to me that attaching the device to the pilings would have the motion detectors aimed across the dock surface at one tide level but aimed above or below the dock surface at the other phases of the tide. I needed the device to remain the prescribed distance above the dock at all times. To accomplish that I built five stands and attached the devices at just the right height above the dock and set them to work. Through the day, solar panels generated the energy and when night came, the alarms were ready to scare the geese away.

This Will Scare Them Away

When I arrived the next morning, the dock was clean. I received reports from other rowers of similar success for the next week. But once again it began with a little poop in spots which grew in time and within a month, we were again having to rely on the pre-launch efforts of our brooms-and-buckets brigade to clean the deck. I don't know how the geese won this one. There must have been places on the dock that the motion detectors didn't cover and even in the areas where they did, if the geese stopped moving the lights and alarms would go off. They also probably realized that there weren't any further consequences beyond the red light and loud alarm. I gave up and signaled my surrender with a white flag on one of the stands to let the geese know they'd won.

Surrender

Happily, goose school moves off the dock after about a month and a half when the goslings begin their flying-south-for-the-winter classes. This experience helped teach me a lesson. Like the human species, other creatures were put on this earth with the ability to make effective adjustments to changes in their circumstances. And our relationship with the "birds of the heavens" and "every living thing that moves on the earth" should not be dominion, but partnership, at least on the Snohomish River.

SEVEN

Regatta

Some of the members of Mill Town Rowing were talking about attending a masters sprint race regatta. I'd watched racing like this on TV. The boats would run side-by-side at top speed along a straight course marked by a string of buoys for 2000 meters. It was nothing like my travels along Steamboat Slough enjoying the sights of bald eagles and harbor seals and I was a little hesitant—actually very hesitant—about participating. I did learn that masters races weren't that long, but breathing hard enough to fuel all the muscles I would be using even for just a 1000 meters was looking pretty painful to me. However, in considering the question over the next few days, my ego took charge and I signed myself up. After all, I was going to be the one in charge of just how much energy I would put into powering my Single.

I could tell that something big was about to happen. My cell phone was filled with text messages from Mill Town rowers participating in the races or just planning to come and watch. Issues of food, housing, and transportation were the main topics of discussion, but the messages also carried a feeling of excitement about the purpose for all that planning.

We all showed up at the boathouse two days before the race. Two Eights, one Quad, two Doubles, and my Single had to be transported to the racecourse. We had to remove all the riggers, lift the boats onto the trailer racks and tie them down. The top racks were probably 10 feet off the ground, so I was happy that there were a number younger and stronger rowers there to do that heavy lifting. Derigged and wrapped in her canvas cover, *Molly* was loaded onto the trailer alongside her big cousins. All the oars and a mountain of equipment also had to be put in the trailer and tied down and I was able to help with that. All this took us over an hour to accomplish and I had occasion several times to consider that at the regatta site, the boats would have to be unloaded from the trailer and rerigged. And at the end of the regatta the boats would have to be derigged again and, with all the rest of the equipment, put on the trailer for the ride home; where they would once more be taken down from trailer, rerigged and returned their homes in the boathouse. It made me wonder whether this racing business was going to be worth all this effort.

I knew we weren't going to be the only club to be racing, but, on arrival at the site of the regatta I was amazed to see all the trailers as big as ours, and bigger, that had showed up and the hundreds of rowers involved in the countless duties that needed to be done. I readied *Molly* and helped the other rowers in our group to rig the other boats. I was glad someone told me to bring a camping chair because even after all the preparations were complete, there was going to be some time to wait between our club's races.

My race was at 1:26 p.m. with plenty of the time before the race to worry about all the things I was going to have to do right. Our women's Eight rowers had the first race and I got a reprieve from my anxiety in joining the other club members cheering them on to an easy victory. But it wasn't long before it was my turn to launch. My worries about launching abruptly evaporated when club members picked up *Molly* and carried her to the launching dock and it wasn't long and I found myself pushed away from the dock and heading out to the warmup area.

Not having spent much of my life in physically competitive activities,

I spent most of my warmup time resting up for the exertion to come. There was some wind and the waves were a bit annoying so I did make some effort to adjust my stroke to avoid slapping the waves on the recovery. It seemed like I was out there a long time waiting for my race, but in actual time it was only 20 minutes. My age group was called to the starting line and when we were all lined up and aimed down the course, I heard "Attention," saw the red flag raised, and on "Go" I was off, down my lane between two strings of small white buoys.

I began with ten quick strokes from half-slide to get off as fast as possible, then lengthening to a full-slide, I worked up to a speed of seven and a half miles per hour and a rate of 30 strokes per minute. Molly and I settled into a rhythm. Drive: from the catch, push hard with my legs; then pull hard with my arms while breathing out hard; then pull hard with my back while breathing in easy. Release: pull the oars out of the water and feather while breathing out easy. Recover: reach forward, bend forward; then slide forward and set the oars at the catch while breathing in hard. Drive, release, and recover, drive, release, and recover, drivel, release, and recover, again and again and again and again......

It seemed like a long way, but I finally passed that single red lane buoy that signaled the halfway mark. But there was still 500 meters to go. I was now rowing at 26 strokes per minute and my speed had dropped. I could see that I was not taking a full slide and focused for the next series of strokes to be sure that my sliding seat made it all the way to the end of the track in the recovery, and my speed did revive a little. Not sure whether it was the result of the wind or bad navigation, but I had drifted over to the starboard side of my lane and when my oar hit one of the lane buoys, I had to make a special effort to get my course straightened out.

My chest and stomach were feeling heavy and my energy level was diminishing, so I was relieved to see the color of the lane buoys change from white to red marking the last quarter of the race. I still had 250 meters to go and had to stay in the rhythm. Drive: from the catch, push hard with my legs; then pull hard with my arms while breathing out hard; then pull hard with my back while breathing in easy. Release:

pull the oars out of the water and feather while breathing out easy. Recover: reach forward, bend forward; then slide forward and set the oars at the catch while breathing in hard. Drive, release, and recover, drive, release, and recover.

Crossing the finish line I immediately stopped rowing. After a few heavy deep breaths, I dropped my head, and didn't move. *Molly* coasted along with the oars drawing wave lines in the water. Once again I wondered to myself whether my five-minute race in the half hour total time on the water could be worth the physical stress I had experienced and all the work and worry I had invested. I received my first answer during the final hundred meters of the race from all the cheers I was hearing from my fellow club members, even though they could all see that I wasn't going to add to the list of medals that many of them had won. That feeling of belonging only grew with all the individual hugs and congratulations I received upon reaching land.

There are a lot of good things about rowing regattas. It's a competition where strength and technique get rewarded. In a team boat you can add teamwork with the other rowers. There are no professional leagues with high paid stars creating a hard line between the faster and slower rowers. Although our club doesn't race against the Washington Husky crew, we often find ourselves on the same water with them. The competitions for women and girls is valued equally with that for men and boys and there are many mixed races both men and women on the same boat. In 2023, 11,000 people showed up and rowed in the Head of the Charles. The smaller regatta that I rowed in still had well over 300 people rowing.

I am not going to stop rowing on the river with the geese, eagles, and seals, but being included in a club of people so connected to one another by the joy of rowing and part of worldwide celebration of the art will draw me to another regatta down the road.

Together at the Regatta

EIGHT

On My Own

Water was an essential partner in the creation of life and has remained indispensable to all of life's evolving forms ever since. I have always had a particular fondness for its oceans, lakes, and rivers, sailing a boat from Hawaii to Seattle, chartering sailboats in Greece, Thailand, Australia, New Zeeland, Norway and the Caribbean, and cruising in sail and power boats for many years in the San Juans Islands, up into British Columbia waters as far as Port Hardy, and in Alaska. Any continuation of those expeditions will be in the hands of my sons, but rowing on the Snohomish River is, and is going to be for as long as possible, a central part of my life.

Winter

It has been snowing and I have been locked in my house watching reruns of M*A*S*H. The club rowing practices had been cancelled because of the snow that covered the boathouse apron, ramp, and dock. Other rowers had intelligently decided to remained away. If a rower were to slip while carrying a boat down to the dock there is a real possibility of damage to the boat and serious injury to the rower. But binge-watching TV has ceased to satisfy my soul and I needed to get out of the house and onto the water. I felt I could avoid that danger of slipping with the procedure I had developed with my dolly because I would never have to lift the boat.

There was no one around when I pulled into the parking area and mine were the only footprints to approach the boathouse. I got *Piper* loaded on the dolly and packed with gear, and walked her through the snow down the ramp onto the dock. My dolly served its purpose and I was able to launch without incident and head upriver.

I was the only thing moving on the river and the gray sky wasn't helping me to deal with the piece of loneliness I was carrying. The Amtrak passenger train sped down the tracks on the west side of the river, but the thought of those passengers sitting warm and comfortably out of the world I was in only made that load a little heavier.

Tree: Silhouette and Reflection

But once under the I-5 Bridge I was pleased to see that group of seagulls I often find there, floating along dipping their heads and flapping their wings in the water. It is interesting that I find them so often in the same place. The only thing unique about that particular spot on the river is the wastewater treatment plant that empties its treated water there. Do the seagulls like it there because the treatment had made the water warmer or less muddy than what was coming down the river from the mountains? I don't know but it was nice to see them there. I found further justification for being here, rowing past the dark shape of a large tree with its leafless branches standing out against the glowing white clouds and reflected in the glassy calm water.

Seagulls Dipping

It is one of the penalties for rowing in winter, my fingers were getting numb. It was a cold day and pulling on the oars compresses the blood vessels in a rower's hands limiting the flow of warm blood to the fingers that our side of the animal spectrum relies on. It made me think of Howard Blackburn, a halibut fisherman in the 1880s who got separated from his mother ship and had to row to shore. His fingers felt numb too, but by the time he had rowed the four days it took to get there, his fingers had become frozen solid, later to be lost to dry gangrene.[3] If Blackburn could survive his cold fingers, I could learn to live with mine.

---

3 Joseph Garland, *Lone Voyager: The Extraordinary Adventures of Howard Blackburn Hero Fisherman of Gloucester* (New York, 1963).

I always like to go down Steamboat Slough. There is less current and the waves are smaller than in the river and it is only a short distance into the Slough until nature takes over the surroundings. I had been staying out of there because it had been duck season and the Slough is a favorite area for the hunters. But it was February and the hunting season had just closed. Looking forward to paying another visit., I turned hard to port out of the River into the Slough hoping to come across something new.

The flotilla on the "Hospice Docks" was unchanged. I'd seen most of those boats moored there for years, several as long as I have been rowing on the Slough. A little further on, that barge and crane abandoned years ago (Chapter V) was still there washed up on the east shore. But from there, it was a short row past one more dock, Holmes Landing, then both sides of the river became completely in the hands of Mother Nature.

It was my plan to row to Eagle Tree, one of the larger evergreen trees on the west side of the waterway. I had named the tree because I had so often seen eagles on its branches standing watch over their nest concealed in the neighboring tree. I am particularly fond of the bald eagle. It always presents itself as an image of strength, no wonder why our Founding Fathers selected it over Ben Franklin's turkey to be our national bird. The bald eagle had suffered from the wide use of DDT, poisoning its food supply and interfering with its ability to produce strong eggshells. Aware of that history left me happily surprised back in 1980 on a boat trip into British Columbia with my young family when we saw a sign of their revival, a series of eagles in the trees about a hundred yards apart searching the waters for their next meal. Seeing an eagle over the Snohomish River always brings back a memory of that early stage in the return of that magnificent bird.

I hadn't been seeing eagles on Eagle Tree for a couple of years and had concluded the family had moved on. However, as I arrived on this day, two eagles flew out of that nest, circled in the air, and perched on Eagle Tree just where I had seen the older generation on those earlier trips. One of the pair soon flew back to the nest while the other remained on Eagle Tree raising the feather off its body, then shaking them back into place (called rousing).

Eagle Tree

    As I sat watching and hoping that this was the beginning of a new generation of eagles for Eagle Tree, *Piper* floated along away from the scene and I took that as nature's decision to close the curtains on that drama and time for me to head back to the dock.

    The mindset on a return row is always different than when outward bound. You know what remains to be done, you have already seen what there is to be seen and your mind feels free to wander. I can't remember what international crisis it was that I solved rowing home that day, but I did remember getting *Piper* onto the dolly and following the wheel tracks through the snow up the ramp and back to the boathouse, getting back in my car, and heading home with the heater on high.

SPRING

Spring can be the "best of times" and the "worst of times" to go rowing on the Snohomish River. We'd been spoiled with some really nice days when the skies were clear and the water is glassy calm, but to make sure we never forget who is in charge, Mother Nature was now serving up a run of cooler temperatures, clouds, and occasional showers. Having been spoiled by those good days, I was having a hard time getting motivated. It was still going to be cloudy, but the winds had lighted up, today's showers weren't expected until afternoon, and I hadn't been out on a solo row for a while. Hoping the river would serve up some additional inspiration I decided to go.

This was going to be my first row in *Molly* this year. On my last trip in Steamboat Slough, I had noticed that the skunk cabbages had begun to bloom. That has long been my cue each year to take *Piper* home and replace her with *Molly* on my rack in the boathouse. With its more stable hull and self-bailing device, *Piper* was a better ally in big waves and easier to handle in the event of a capsize into the colder water of winter than the more slender and less stable *Molly*. But with spring, there would be less trouble with waves, the water would be warmer, and I was looking forward to rowing faster.

With *Molly* on her dolly, I walked down the ramp and found a heron standing tall at the end of the dock. We often find ourselves sharing our dock with other creatures, a lonely seagull, a pair of Mallard ducks, human fishermen when the salmon are spawning, and of course, the Canada geese (see Chapter VI). For a long moment the heron stood there ignoring my presence looking out across the river, but finally flew off in search of more privacy.

Heron on the Dock

As I proceeded to launch *Molly* I noticed some footsteps imprinted in the layer of dew on the dock. At first I thought they might be steps the heron made earlier before I got there, but looking a little closer I noticed there were five toes, not three, and no talon sticking out behind. I launched *Molly* and headed upriver wondering what kind of a critter left those prints. Some later online research revealed them to be otter prints.

Otter Prints

Out on the river the sun made the thinning clouds glow causing the glassy calm water to reflect like silver. There a was a Canada goose sitting on top of one of the dolphins that stood along the west side of the River having what I guessed was an important family discussion with another goose swimming around in the water below.

As I was getting ready to turn into the Slough, I notice an odd shape struggling in the water. Pulling alongside, I could see there were two Canada geese floating in the water, flapping their wings. The birds were holding onto each other by their beaks. I glided to a stop and watched the two continue their struggle. Finally, one of the birds dove, or was pushed under the water and they separated. When the one bird surfaced it had had enough of the combat and flew away pursued by the other bird, both loudly squawking out their claims of righteousness. With that drama at an end, I headed down the Slough.

Deadheads are a frequent hazard on the Snohomish River and even more so on Steamboat Slough. And springtime when the water runs higher is a time new ones often appear. A log has been drifting around in the river long enough to soak up water and the heavier end, often a tree's root system, sinks down and sticks to the bottom with the lighter end sticking up out of the water. Deadheads are a particular problem for us rear-facing rowers. Even if we know about a particular deadhead, letting the mind drift off into more exciting topics can lead to a collision that can make a hole in the hull or catch an oar and capsize the boat. I have had my encounters with deadheads, but on this day I managed to navigate safely. There is one deadhead I actually look forward to seeing. I call it Hippo. It's looking over at me as I row past dining on a mouth full of grass.

The Hippo Deadhead

    The dominant color along the bank was still brown, but the bare limbs of the trees were showing early signs of budding and some of the early blooming bushes were beginning to show their yellow flowers. The grasses and reeds had begun their new growth and the dead blades and stalks had been washed away, collecting in clumps floating along in the river. I ran through one of these clumps every now and again and would hear the light tapping sound of their contact with the boat's hull. At one point my Speed Coach started reading zero. Some of those grasses had wrapped around the Speed Coach impeller. So, I stopped rowing and preformed a fanny wiggle, pulling hard with my starboard oar then hard with my port oar, to cause the stern of the boat to swing over to one side then the other. The procedure did the trick and the Speed Coach was back in business.

    The clouds had continued to thin and I first became able see the sun appearing as an undefined glow in one spot in the sky. A little later still behind the clouds but peeking through as a glowing orb. My trip down the slough took the sun behind the cover of some trees, but as I arrived into the open area where Ebey Slough flows into Steamboat, the sun appeared again, now surrounded by a halo of light and the colors of the rainbow, a final reward for my day's travels in the Snohomish River Estuary.

BILL JAQUETTE

The Halo

NINE

Still On My Own

Summer

Summertime is a good time to take a special rowing expedition, a trip around Ebey Island. It starts up the River, all the way to the entrance to Ebey Slough, then down Ebey to where it joins Steamboat Slough, through Steamboat back to the River and down to the dock, a trip of 15.3 miles. That's going to take a while and I better get going early to avoid the afternoon heat.

The water conditions were perfect: the river was moving slowly and the complete absence of wind left the water glassy smooth, a mirror reflection of the blue sky and the trees along the river. The mountains were out, but with their summertime loss of snow, and viewed through the summer haze, they did not dominating the scene as they could in winter. Arriving at the boathouse I loaded up all the necessities: a Speed Coach to record my speed and distance through the water; a runner's GPS to record my speed and distance along the shore; my waterproof camera for any encounter with some nice scenery; my cellphone (See Chapter IV); and my seat pad. Down to the water I launched *Molly* and headed upriver. The juniors were scheduled for an outing and I was pleased to have gotten out of the way before they arrived.

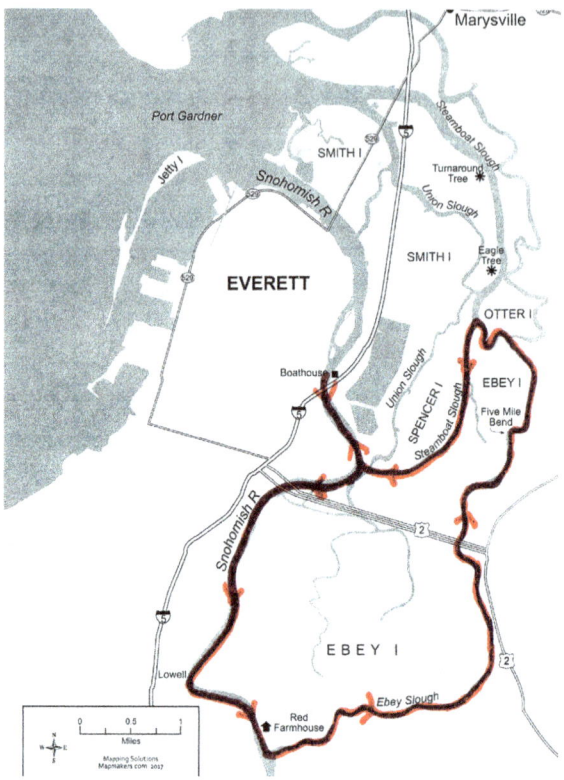

Circumnavigating Ebey Island

The first three miles of this trip were familiar territory. I rowed past the entry to Steamboat Slough on starboard then a little further along the collection of unused commercial fishing boats tied up on Everett's river harbor on port. From there I traveled under the Hwy 2 Bridge and past all the new apartments on the west side of the river. The homeless camp was still there, as were the cows grazing at the river's edge wondering what this strange thing was coming up the river splashing something into the water again and again and again.

The high voltage powerlines crossing the river came next. This is a favorite place for our masters practice sessions to spin around and row back to the dock. It makes a high overhead finish line for the three and a half mile pull against the river current. It was just a start for my row today, but I did stop for a rest and was pleased to see a bald eagle sitting high up on the eastern transmission tower.

Curious Cows

It was not far to the community of Lowell where the river turns east. Rotary Park is on what has become the south side of the river. There are two people casting lines out into the river from its shore and several people launching kayaks at the boat ramp. A little further on I pass a large cement dam-like structure, the controlling gate for the seven-mile-long Marshland Canal, built to control flooding in the farming area south of the River. It isn't far to the red farmhouse that looks out over the river from the north shore and then into Ebey Slough.

The entrance to Ebey Slough is quite shallow and deadheads like to collect there. I proceeded with caution but the current took charge and carried *Molly* right over a sunken deadhead that I could see in the water right underneath us. Luckily the water was deep enough and we passed over it without any contact.

Once fully into Ebey the rowing became easy. We were in farm country and, although I could see several large barns, the rower's vantage point below the riverbank wasn't giving me a view of any of the activity on land, so I focused on my rowing.

Any boat on the move leaves a trail of scrambled water behind it.

A rower must invest their energy in a number of other ways, including what it takes to gain movement through the air and to overcome the friction of the oarlock and sliding seat. But the energy it takes to cause that scrambling is the price we pay for movement through the water, and one of the rewards of rowing is seen in the subtlety of that disturbance in comparison to the waves made by almost any other kind of vessel. Glancing at that trail made me look for the sun. It wasn't going to work right now, but around the next bend, I was able to aim *Molly*'s stern in the direction of the sun and the scrambled water becomes a blinking light show.

Trail of Sparkling Light

As always happens with things going smoothly I start to think about other things. That has cost me some near misses, and a few actual contacts with floating logs and deadheads, but I can't help it. I started to think about a comment I got the other day from another rower in a Quad with me, asking me, in a nice way, to stop looking around. The rower explained that staying focused on the motions of the rower in front of me would keep me better synchronized with the other rowers.

On shore the coach explained that on something as slender as a racing shell, looking around can also put the boat out of balance. Well, I didn't need to worry about synchronizing with anyone, but I thought I would test the question of balance. Looking over to my left did make the boat tip ever so slightly that way; looking to my right tipped the boat slightly the other way. Although the boat remained on course and was never in danger I could feel that I was having to make small adjustments with my oars to keep the boat balanced. I was never going to give up looking around. What can be seen looking around on the Snohomish River is a big reason I was out here, but I promised myself when rowing in a team boat I would—well most of the time—stay focused on those rowers in front of me. Today, however, was a day for sightseeing.

On a glance to my right I saw a coyote searching the beach for something tasty. They tell me that there are coyotes living all over this area. But they must be good at staying concealed because I have had only two other sightings in all my time rowing on the Snohomish.

Coyote

I'd made good progress down Ebey Slough, passing through open farmland, and was now finding more trees along the shore. In my forward-view mirror, I saw some movement in the water, and glided to a stop to check it out. A beaver was swimming in my direction. I just sat there as motionless as possible, but when the beaver got close enough and realized that I was something out of the ordinary, it slapped its tail in the water and dove. I waited for it to surface again, but it must have managed to slip up the bank under cover and I moved along.

It wasn't far to the Hwy 2 bridge with all of the mud birds' nests underneath on its support beams. Last spring, I must have seen a hundred sparrows there caring for those nest and their babies inside. On that trip, many of them flew off and circled in the air as I passed through. This time through I could still see the nests, but their purpose had been served for this year and the birds were no longer there.

Another boat-hospice facility came next, with some very tired boats tied up to the dock. Although there were none there today, this area had been the graveyard for a number of sunken boats on my travels in the past. It was a short run to Five Mile Bend, a turn of the Slough that, according to my GPS device, is almost exactly five miles from the dock where we launch. I have often used this as my turnaround spot when coming the other way. Today it served as a point of relief, a message to my body that the rest of the trip was doable.

Doable yes, but I needed to get going. I rowed past Otter Island on my starboard, turned to port into Steamboat Slough where I took a long drink of water and a five-minute rest. I knew I was getting tired because the number of miles yet to go kept popping into my head: two miles up the Steamboat, then one mile down the River. But the current against me in the Slough was light and in the River strongly in my favor and it didn't take too long before I found myself with *Molly* alongside the dock, but completely exhausted. The river current had cut down the distance I had had to row through the water by a mile, but it had still been a long way.

The dock was littered with shoes and I realized that the juniors were still on the water. Looking downriver, I saw the girls and boys Eights come into view moving fast and decided I better find the energy to get moving again. I managed to get *Molly* on to her rack and was walking to my car when the juniors appeared carrying their boats up the ramp. I headed home where I didn't leave the couch for the rest of the day.

The Junior Rowers Left Their Shoes Behind

Fall

Nighttime has caught up with the daylight, so it must be fall. I had spent a lot of my summer rowing in club practice sessions, much of it focused on preparing to race, keeping in mind the requirement to keep my eyes focused directly aft. So I was thinking that a more leisurely row would be best this time out. The fall rains had been coming and going, and I hadn't been able to schedule a perfectly calm and cloudless day. This morning's weather forecast was calling for clouds with rain on the way. At least the winds were to be light, so with rain forecast for the rest of the week, I decided this was the day to go.

The older I get, the longer it takes to get the stiffness of the night's sleep out of my body. I spent my first half hour of consciousness drinking my instant coffee and working to generate the body movement I was going to need just to make it down to the boathouse. It became time to go, I overruled the objection from the small of my back and headed down to the river.

I opened the boathouse and started preparing *Molly* for another day on the water. It was the time of the year to switch my boats, bring *Piper* back for safer rowing in fall and winter and take *Molly* home for several coats of wax and, after today, a good rest. Heading down to the dock for *Molly's* last row of the year, I saw three harbor seals out on the breakwater logs. I'd often seen these same characters, or maybe their understudies, in these same locations during the winter and spring. It must mean that the water is getting colder.

Seals on the Breakwater Logs

I wasn't surprised to find several fishermen on the dock casting their lines out into the river. I felt a little awkward interrupting their quest, but as always they were cordial and completely accommodating, and wished me well as I rowed away. It turned out that we were not the only species aware the salmon were spawning. On one of the dolphins on the west side of the river, there was an eagle chomping away on the remains of a salmon. An osprey was perched on a light pole waiting its turn and the two harbor seals that popped their heads out of the water behind the boat were no doubt there for the same reason. Nearing the entrance to the Slough I approached a salmon swimming slowly along with its dorsal fin protruding out of the water. When it didn't dart away I knew it had already spawned and was just drifting in the current waiting to die. With no interest in the salmon, a flock of Canada geese flew overhead in their V formation, training their new generation for the flight south later in the year. As I approached a large group of sparrows that had been perched in the trees, they all flew up and around and around over the water, a mini-murmuration. After circling for a while, they realized I was neither a friend nor enemy and flew back into the trees.

The flora along the shore were beginning to show their fall colors. The leaves on some trees were still green, others well on their way to brown. The bushes were showing their varying shades of red and yellow and the entire show was mirrored in the glassy calm water. I wouldn't put it up against New England's fall colors, but still a uniquely inspiring place to be on the water.

Fall Colors

A short time later I noticed something swimming around in the water. Most of the time that turns out to be a seal and, with the salmon spawning, there were certainly a lot of seals around. But this looked a little different, so I swung around and drifted to a stop and get a closer look. From its manner of travel I thought it might be an otter. There are otters living in the Slough, but they are very private and I have often been fooled by a seal that is just carrying its head lower in the water.

But seals tend to just pop up and look casually around and this creature appeared to be on a mission. I watched as it headed across the Slough. Maybe it was because it noticed me, but for some reason it suddenly dove sticking its spiked tail out of the water rewarding my patience and confirming my suspicion that it was an otter.

Approaching the entrance to Ebey Slough I saw something strange in my forward-view mirror, a pure white bird on tall legs walking around on the muddy shore. I spun around to look at it directly. It was an egret, a bird I'd seen in other places, but never in the Snohomish River estuary. Had global warming made the Northwest a fit habitat for egrets? Well no, I guess that bird's report back to the flock must not have been favorable and I haven't had other egret sightings since.

The Egret

Well, "a leisurely row" had been the order of the day, so I turned around and headed back to the dock with all my rewards for that day. As I neared the end, the rain that had been forecast arrived, Mother Nature's way of politely telling me it was time to get off her river. The fishermen were just packing up to leave when I landed, but one did stop to show me the nice salmon he had caught while I was out. *Molly* was dollied up the ramp and into the boat house and I went home happy with my leisurely row and full permission to look around all I wanted.

TEN

ONE MORE

I'd been spending time away from the River at rowing regattas with Mill Town Rowing and had not been rowing the 83.33 miles per month I need to reach 1000 miles in the year. And the late fall weather this year hadn't been helpful. I'd been knocking out miles when I could, but it was December 28—that's actually winter, isn't it—and I still had nine miles to go. According to the several weather sources, the storm the day before had passed and the next wave wasn't going to arrive until late morning. The following three days were going to keep me busy off the water, so I needed to get going.

Driving to the boathouse I saw the clouds moving fast overhead, but there was no wind on the river—yet! I loaded *Piper* with all of the equipment needed for a solo trip and dollied her down to the dock to find two harbor seals occupying the far end of the dock. They must have felt comfortable because they sat their at their ease while I launched and rowed away.

Who's the Guest on This Dock?

We were on the way to an exceptionally high tide, often called a King Tide, and the water was flowing upriver, helping me along. Passing under the I-5 Bridge I found the wind calm and the river glassy smooth. With all the rain we've been having, the high level of the water has washed several logs that had spent the summer ashore out into the river and they had been washing down stream in the normal river flow, but back upstream in the incoming tide. In my forward-view mirror, I saw one that I'd seen before and pulled over to avoid it.

One of Many on the Snohomish

About a half a mile along I felt a brisk gust of wind blow by me and saw it darken the water with wavelets as it passed. I had paid almost no attention to that, until a second gust of wind a little stronger and much longer blew by. Those were easy to manage but it made me consider going down Steamboat Slough where the channel receives some protection because of all the trees along its bank. It was duck hunting season and I usually stay out of the Slough from November 1st to January 31st. But it was a weekday. I thought that and the bad weather forecast would keep most of the hunters away. Anyway, I had my airhorn tapped to the rigger so I decided to take the chance.

I knew I had to get down Steamboat at least to Turnaround Tree to be sure to get in the nine miles I needed. I could tell that the wind was getting stronger, but the water remained calm except where the Slough bent around parallel with the direction of the wind.

One loud shot rang out and, after a momentary break, two more shots in quick succession. Almost immediately a duck, hurriedly flapping its wings, flew out across the river and into the trees on the other side. I couldn't see the hunter and no shotgun pellets hit the waters of the Slough. I reasoned that the shots were aimed the other way over the Spencer Island Swamp that lies west of the Slough. To make sure, I pressed my airhorn, three short blasts, three long blasts, then three more short blasts: SOS, the only Morse Code I knew. At least the hunter would know that some human was on the Slough. The shooting stopped for the time being and I rowed on.

The clouds were getting more dramatic and the wind gusts had become a steady wind, but I had a ways to go to be sure that the whole trip would give me the full nine miles. Past the entrance to Ebey Slough, the channel bent around parallel to the wind and I could feel that the wind had gotten stronger. I did manage to add that next mile down to Turnaround Tree and head back.

The dark shapes crossing the water accompanying the gusts of wind were more frequent and I could often feel *Piper* roll to the side when the gusts arrived. While still in the Slough the waves were manageable but I became concerned what it was going to be like when I got to the River.

I stopped to rest at the entrance to the Slough. Looking out into the River I could see the white-capping waves. There was no other way back to the dock, so I headed out into probably the roughest water I had ever experienced in the Snohomish Estuary. Generated by the strong south wind the waves were made taller against the still inflowing current. *Piper* was pitching forward and backward and I kept striking the waves with my oars on the recovery. The incoming current was not only helping to build the waves but was causing me to row further through the water than I was progressing along the shore. Water was splashing into the cockpit leaving me soaked from the waist down. It didn't occur to me at the time, but that was some cold late fall water the river was throwing at me. *Piper* did have a self-bailing cockpit, so the water washed aboard was being drained out through the device. My SpeedCoach was showing *Piper* at about four mph when moving down the back of a wave and down to less than three when moving up the front of a wave.

Because I knew the wind, waves, and cold water would have made a self-rescue from a capsize very difficult, I was being very cautious. Moving all the way down the sliding seat on the recovery left the boat feeling tippy, so I would frequently slide only partway down or sometimes not at all before getting ahold of the water with the oars to perform the drive. It was slow-going but I was making progress and at one point I looked at the SpeedCoach and saw that I had rowed the nine miles I needed for my thousand miles in the year. Now if I can only make it back to the dock, I would have something to celebrate.

Passing under the I-5 Bridge, I knew there was only a quarter of a mile to go. The bend in the river left me in the calmer waves that did not have the long run in which to build and I rowed with more confidence to the dock. With a great sense of relief I lifted *Piper* onto the dolly and rolled her up the ramp and into the boathouse. I drove home pleased that I had made it a thousand miles in another year and spent the evening at home thinking of the rowing I was going to be doing in the next year under better conditions in the Snohomish River.

Still Rowing on the Snohomish

I'll Be Out There Again Next Year

PART 2

ELEVEN

Winter

It is still dark, but I have to get to work, and winter is late with its morning light. I caught the weather on the TV, and it's going to be cold and cloudy, but the rain is not due until afternoon, and it's a definite time to go. This time of year, I won't be the first person to the Everett Rowing Association boathouse; the Morning Glory rowing group will be there for their 6:00 a.m. workout on the rowing machines. The sun will rise at 7:52, which, if I push it a bit, will allow me to hit the water at about 7:20 with enough light to be able to see where I am going. During the winter, I am going to be rowing my more-stable Maas 24 scull. She is named *Piper*, a name used for boats by three generations of my family. I always thought of it as a very nice woman's name but have recently figured out that the name might have come into use because my grandfather smoked a pipe.

It is cold enough that part of me is looking for an excuse to turn around and go home and get on the stair stepper in my warm house, but as usual, the effort to gather up my rowing gear and drive to the boathouse creates enough momentum that the other part of me wins the debate. I rig the boat and take the oars and water bottle to the dock. The part of the Snohomish River we row on is affected by tide, and the speed and direction of the current in the river will vary substantially. It is still fairly dark, but in the reflection of some lights from across the river, I can see that I will be dealing with a strong downstream current. My row upstream is going to be slower, but if the tide doesn't change, it will be a quick trip home.

There is frost on the dock, and I have this vision of falling with the boat on top of me, so it is important to go slowly. All goes well. I lift the boat into the water, put in the oars, shift myself onboard, and shove off. Those first strokes feel a little awkward; have I forgotten how to do this? No, I just need to get the boat moving; it stabilizes, and I am away. It is still twilight, but the dim light of predawn and the reflections in the water make me happy to have gotten away and not be part of the roar of the traffic I hear on the bridge overhead.

Rowing a scull is a very efficient form of movement. The nine-and-a-half-foot oars provide great leverage for pulling against the water and the required stabilizing for the very slender and fast hull. The sliding seat allows me to add the power of the legs to that of the arms and back. It is exhilarating to be able to travel so swiftly and efficiently with such little disturbance of the water.

Piper

As I move upriver, it gets lighter and lighter, and the reflection in the water turns from blue to silver. The branches of trees begin to stand out clear against the gray sky. The seagulls resting in the river wait until the last second to move out of my way.

I have some choices where to go, stay on the river or head down Steamboat Slough. It is duck-hunting season, and you can often hear gunfire on the slough. But it's a weekday, and there won't be as many hunters out, so I decide to try the slough. Once I get past that old marina, the slough takes me out into nature. Although hidden in the clouds, the sun is now fully up. I can see the trees along the bank showing clearly in the water against the silver reflection of the gray sky.

Uh-oh, gunfire. I have never felt that I was down range from shots being fired, but it still makes me a little nervous. I carry a small air horn that I tape to the boat during hunting season; I give it three blasts to make sure that the hunters know I am here.

There are always birds around. It is still early winter, and it seems as if they are mostly just hanging out, waiting for spring. Over there, I see a lone bald eagle perched high on a bare tree. A little later on, I see two others sitting next to one another, one looking out over the river toward the hills to the east. There seem to be more eagles around in the winter. Perhaps that is because they are more visible when the trees are bare; perhaps they are just hanging out and waiting for some food source to come back elsewhere. There goes another one flying far overhead and landing in the tree over there. Swimming along, up ahead I can see a pair of common mergansers, the male in black and white and the gray female with its red hood. They are smart not to be flying high this time of year.

I have named a number of locations on the river as places to turn around and head back. Today I row past Eagle Tree, named by me because it is the most reliable place to see eagles on my route on Steamboat Slough. I used this as my turnaround objective for a number of years. I don't have any early appointments; I think I'll go to Turnaround Tree. Passing Eagle Tree and heading on to Turnaround Tree, it comes to mind that every stroke I row now means a longer trip and more strokes to get me back. So it is just a bit of relief to turn around and head back now with an idea of how much energy it is going to take.

Eagle Tree

Out rowing by myself is a good time for thinking. Once the requirements for a powerful stroke and the necessities for keeping my balance passed from my conscious brain to my unconscious brain, rowing became a good time for thinking. The rhythmic use of the body's muscles producing that quiet and efficient movement through the water helps to keep what is going on in the conscious brain in balance too.

Turnaround Tree

Thump, I hit a log. The momentum carries the boat up on top of it. The collision causes a knot in my left thigh muscle. Fortunately, it is not a large log, and the boat slides on over, only banging again when the log hits the skeg. As I knead the knot out of my muscle, I think back to a run-in with a much bigger log when the boat did not pass over but got stuck on top with my weight positioned right over the log, crushing the boat. I remember well the sound of the cracking fiberglass. I did make it back to the dock that day, filling with water as I went, but the boat had to go in for substantial repairs.

I have a mirror on my hat like bicyclists wear, which allows me to keep an eye forward, but the thinking I so enjoy distracted me from keeping watch. I remind myself to stay aware from here on. Good thing I remember that deadhead that planted itself just about here a couple of weeks ago. There it is. I pull over to the side of the river to pass.

I am getting close to home. Looking around, I see that the clouds have lifted a little. I can see the foothills to the east showing some fresh snow. Clouds still hide the mountains beyond; getting a look at them will have to wait for another day.

I'm moving fast now. The current in the main river makes it a quick part of the trip, and I pass the dock, make a U-turn, and pull up. I sit there for a moment, have a drink of water, take out the oars and climb out. Pulling the boat out of the water and hoisting it onto my shoulders is a significant exertion, a little tougher now because of the nine miles I have just rowed. Walking up the ramp with *Piper* on my shoulder focuses my eyes on a large white alder tree across the road at the top. It is now bare, but I anticipate the varying visions it will present to me over the course of the year. At the top, I put the boat on the slings and go back to the dock to retrieve the oars and my water bottle. It takes me a few minutes to wipe the boat down and put her back on her rack in the boathouse. Now I am off to work.

Welcoming Alder in Winter

~

In winter, I always look at the outdoor thermometer I have at my house before leaving for a row. For the last few days, it has been unusually cold, into the single digits. If other factors are favorable, I will row in the teens, but the single digits kept me onshore. Today looks doable, no wind and no rain. The temperature is in the high twenties, and it's Saturday, so I can wait until the sun is fully up.

I launch and head out but soon encounter something new to me, a patch of thin ice floating down the river. I pull to the side and easily avoid it. However, not far along, I encounter another, larger patch that I can't avoid. The ice is very thin, and *Piper* manages to move through without too much difficulty. The oars chop into the ice, which provides firmer than usual points to pull against, and I am soon back into fluid water.

There seem to be more sheets of ice flowing in my direction in the faster current in the main river, and I decide to head down Steamboat Slough. A few hundred yards down the slough, I see that this was a mistake. The calmer water in the slough has allowed the ice to form from one bank to the other. It is still thin, and I can chop my way along, but this isn't fun, and I turn around and head back.

Just as I reach the main river, an eagle swoops overhead within twenty feet; moments later, it does it again. I soon realize that it isn't me that the eagle is after; it's a duck swimming along about thirty feet behind me. The winter months have forced the eagles away from their normal fish diet to other sources of food. As the eagle swoops down, the duck dives under the water to avoid the attack. When the duck surfaces, the eagle swoops in again. I am afraid that the duck is going to become exhausted from the continual diving and, forced to remain at the surface to catch an extra breath, will get caught in the eagle's attack. Perhaps disturbed by my presence, and fortunately for the duck, the eagle gives up and flies off to a nearby light pole.

To make up for the row I was missing, I rowed a ways downriver past the dock. Here, the river water mixes with the saltwater in Port Gardner Bay, and ice is not a problem. I row a couple of miles down to the industrial sites along the river, turn around, and head back. I am going to remember that strategy the next time I encounter ice.

It rains a lot in the wintertime in the Northwest. In Seattle on average, it rains on more days than it doesn't from November through March. However, rainy fronts often pass through in short order, leaving plenty of opportunities for a dry row. Every now and again, however, you just have to row in the rain. After all, it is just water. Well, today is one of those days. The forecast the night before offered hope of a little break, but the early-morning TV meteorologist let me know that the front had come in early. Any chance of talking myself out of going disappeared when I saw that the Everett Rowing Club had put together a group of hearty master rowers for a morning row. At least it is calm. As I launch, I can see the rain hitting the water. Most of the drops hit the water like tiny pebbles, but occasionally drops will roll around the surface for a brief moment like a tiny, clear marble.

Masters Rowers Launching

It is a weekend, and I can hear the hunters, so I decide to stay in the river and row up past the city of Everett's river harbor. Shortly after leaving the dock, I meet the other rowers. They have turned around and are headed back to the warm and dry of the clubhouse. The low clouds and the insistent rain make me feel a bit lonely. It is heartening to see two large harbor seals lying up on a rotting log boom. They turn and lift up their heads just enough to watch me row past.

Harbor Seals Getting Out of the Cold Water

An eagle sitting on a tree behind them sees something in the water, swoops down, and grabs a hold of it. It starts to lift it out of the water, but whatever that was is too heavy, and the eagle is forced to let go and fly back to its perch in the tree. Once past the harbor, there is farmland to the east. On the other side of the river, I see the blue tarps and other gear of the several homeless encampments. My time out in the wet and cold will be over in an hour. That allows me to find pleasure and satisfaction being out here. I cannot imagine how it would be to have no escape.

Homeless Camp

We had some heavy rain over the last few days, and the river has been quite full. That means that there are probably some logs to watch out for. There is one now, right in the middle of the river. The limbs are gone, but the root system rises out of the water menacingly. I row far over to the side of the river to pass it. I need to remember this guy when I head back down river. You can encounter all sorts of floating hazards on the Snohomish River. There are some old logs that have been around for a while. I am guessing that they had spent time washed up onshore, but the rising water level has launched them once again to float up and down stream with the incoming and outgoing tides until coming ashore when the rain lets up and the river returns to its normal levels.

I have made it to the sharp bend in the river at the community of Lowell and now turn around and head back. The rain hasn't let up, and I am very wet. The evaporation of the water, even on the outside of my raincoat, is cooling me off. So it is time to finish the row. Fortunately, I am now traveling with the current and moving along nicely. I pass that log, which has kindly floated over to one side of the river. Before long, I am back at the dock. As I carry my boat up the ramp, I can see, as I suspected, that mine is the only car left in the lot. In order to get my boat dry, I have to set up slings inside the boathouse. No reason to hang around. I put things away and drive home, remembering to sit on a plastic bag to keep the car's seat dry.

~

Every now and again during winter, you get one of those days—clear, cold, and calm. This is one of those days. It is well below freezing—time to dress in my warmest outfit, bring that extra heavy vest, and be sure to wear the beanie under my hat. As I drive to the boathouse, I can see, against the barely lit sky, the dark shapes of the mountains to the east, Whitehorse and Three Fingers standing out over the rest. The temperature of the air is twenty-one degrees, which is just about half the temperature of the water in the river. There is frost all over, so it is important to walk carefully while carrying *Piper* and, particularly, to remember to take baby steps when I get to the slippery dock. As I put *Piper* into the water, a bird flies up and lands on one of the nearby pilings. In this very early-morning light, I can only see its shape, but I can tell that it is some kind of a hawk. It gives me a quick look and flies away. I climb aboard, and I too am away.

It hasn't rained much in the last couple of days, and the cold temperature means that the snow is staying in the mountains, so the current isn't particularly strong. I need to stay alert for the logs that have been moving up and down the river with the changing currents, and I am sure that the high tide will have lifted those two deadheads and moved them to rest somewhere new. However, the visibility is good, and the rising sun is making it better every minute, so navigation isn't going to be a problem.

I have the cold under control except for my hands. My light bike gloves do nothing to keep my hands warm, and the pulling on the oars inhibits the flow of warming blood into my fingers. It is going to take a while, but eventually the capillaries in my hands will expand from the increasing blood pressure of my exercise, and I will begin to feel a burning in my fingers as they begin to get warm.

With the full sun, everything brightens. Every branch of the leafless alder trees, even the smallest twig, is covered with frost glowing bright white against the blue sky, all reflecting in the calm river. It brightens my mood, and it looks to have done the same for the eagle perched proudly on the high branch of that tree. The hunting season is over, so it is safe to head down Steamboat Slough, and there are more eagles and even one hawk to be seen. Heading down the slough, I can see Mount Olympus and the rest of the Olympic range, only to see it disappear as I pass the next bend in the river. As the river turns, Mount Rainier briefly appears in the distance. Winter is the best time for mountain viewing; there is more snow, and there is not the haze that you see in the summer.

Eagle in Frosty Tree

  Well, here I am at Turnaround Tree. Time to turn around. I dig the port oar into the water, and the boat begins to pivot around. Ten strokes with my starboard oar complete the turn, and I am headed back. As I row back up the slough, I can see Mount Baker behind me to the north, a brilliant white in the sun. One of the ever-present harbor seals pops its head out of the water, gives me a quick glance, and moves on. The rowing has been uneventful, and it will continue to be if I remember to stay to the right when passing that deadhead about half of the way back to the main river.

  Once in the main river, it is a quick trip with the current back to the boathouse. On landing, I notice that the water that splashed up on the deck during my row has frozen, and there are icicles hanging from the gunnels, testimony to what *Piper* and I had experienced. The dock is still slippery, and I take particular precautions to remain fully balanced as I pull the boat out of the water and hoist it onto my shoulders. On my way up the ramp with the boat on my shoulder, I focus as always on the white alder tree. It, too, is covered with frost, making this welcome a little bit special. It is Sunday, and it's winter; there has been no one else at the boathouse. I clean up, pack up, and drive home past Three Fingers and Whitehorse Mountains, now in bright sunshine.

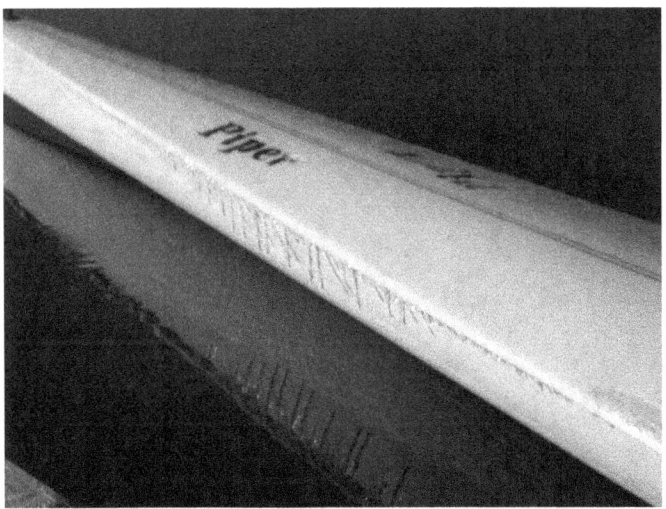

Icicles Hanging from the Gunwale

~

I didn't row yesterday. That was Saturday, usually a good day to go; I can row longer, and there are often others out on the water. But it was windy and raining. I went to the boathouse thinking that I might get inspired to go anyway, but I just couldn't overcome the negative inertia, and I turned around and went home. As the day went on, improving weather provided a growing enticement to get on the water. Today there is a big storm in the forecast, increasing rain showers with winds up to seventy miles per hour during the day, and the TV newscasters are warning us to stay inside and be sure to have plenty of flashlight batteries. However, motivated by the embarrassment of my decision yesterday, I really want to go. If I can get on the water early enough, maybe I can get a row in before things get too bad.

The sky is cloudy as I drive to the boathouse, but those clouds rise as they travel east, revealing the mountains below, appearing in stark black and white. The flags on the several poles along the river give a mixed message about the wind, but there is nothing to overcome my commitment. As I ready *Piper* for the row, I can hear the singing of the frogs in a nearby pond recently awakened from their winter hibernation. I carry the boat down to the water, put her in, and shove off. The weather isn't so bad right now.

Boathouse from an Early-Morning Launch

I hit the water just before high tide, and there is still a bit of an upstream current helping me along. As is my usual choice, I turn down Steamboat Slough. The slough can be a good place to minimize the effect of wind. There are places where the breeze is noticeable, but there are others where the particular angle of the river in relation to the direction of the wind allows the trees along the bank to provide protection. As compensation for my cowardice of yesterday, I decide to row farther than usual, past Turnaround Tree, past the old barn on the west side of the river, down to the far I-5 bridge and back.

In late winter, the dead grasses and reeds detach from the living plants, making room for new growth. Lifted off by the high tides, they wash into the river, where they gather together in bundles. Because the tide is very high right now, there are lots of these bundles on the river. I try to avoid them, but every now and again I pass through a patch; one encounter leaves a long reed caught around my skeg; another encounter wraps one over an oar. Lurking among the reed and grass bundles are some smaller logs, hard to see because they are sitting so low in the water. At the last second, I see one. I dig the oars into the water, bringing the boat to a stop but not fast enough. *Bang*, the bow of the boat hits the log; not too big, the log slips easily under the boat. *Bang* again, it hits the skeg and then slides away.

As I near the end of the row, just as I pass under the near I-5 bridge, I see what looks like my own wake growing larger and now moving up toward me. Reaching just about to my stern, the wave parts, and a large harbor seal rolls out of the water, gives me a quick look, and rolls back into the water. Moments later, it surfaces again and swims casually away. I have had close encounters like this on a number of occasions; more often, it is just a simple glance as I row by. Harbor seals are a constant companion on the river at all times of the year. Even when they don't come in close to me, I sense that they are always aware of my presence. I think they are sensing the movement of the water I cause with my wake and have come by to explore, hoping that I am a big fish.

Rowing to the dock, I notice that the clouds have gotten lower. There is still not a lot of wind, but it is good that I am finishing up now. I land, lift the boat onto my shoulders, and head up the ramp. As I do, it begins to rain—perfect timing. By the time I get home, the wind has come up, and I resolve to heed the warning of the TV newscasters and stay inside for the rest of the day, listening to the wind howl. I was lucky that my power stayed on.

∼

I use my Speed Coach to aid me with my rowing. It has helped me improve and maintain my rowing technique. I will often look down and find that I am going slower than I had hoped and question, *Am I keeping my back straight? Am I not stretching my arms far enough aft before the catch where I dig the oars into the water and begin the pull? Is my stroke not the most efficient coordination of my legs, back, and arms, or do I just need to work harder?*

For me, the Speed Coach is also important for measuring the distance of my rows. In rowing on the river, it is not enough to know how far it is along the river to my turnaround spot. The current makes it a much longer row heading upstream and a much shorter row heading downstream. Along with helping me with my technique, the Speed Coach tells me how far I row through the water.

A couple of years ago, I also started using a runner's GPS watch to track my speed and distance along the land for comparison with the data from my Speed Coach, which measures my speed and distance through the water. Using the two instruments together gives me a good measure of how the currents are affecting my progress. When working against the current, my speed along the land can slow to five, four, or maybe even down to three-plus miles per hour, while my speed through the water remains relatively constant, somewhere between six and seven-plus miles per hour, depending on which boat I am rowing and my energy level at the time. With the current, while rowing at the same speed through the water, my speed along the land can reach eight, nine, and very occasionally ten miles per hour.

There is a lot of variation in the currents on the Snohomish River. The basic flow of the river depends on how much water flows out of the Cascade Mountains. Melting snow can provide a good current, particularly in the spring. A good rain anytime can make the water run fast, brown with soil from upstream. The river current is also affected by the ebb and flood of the tide. An ebb tide will significantly increase the river's flow. A flood tide, particularly after a deep low tide and with greater effect in the summer, when it rains less often and the snow melt is minimal, can produce a substantial upriver current. In seasons when the basic flow is strong, the river might not flow upriver even in a strong flood, but a rower can often find relief from the full force of the downstream current by choosing to row during the flood.

~

It can be hard to find a day to go rowing in winter. Cold weather, except in the extremes, can be accommodated with more layers of clothing, but the rare appearance of ice in the river, and the more common strong winds and heavy rains can make it difficult to schedule a time to go out or add to the difficulty when I do. However, on those days that really aren't so pleasant, I can usually congratulate myself for just getting out there, and every winter does have those occasional days that are truly rewarding.

TWELVE

Spring

I am not waiting for the equinox; it's spring. My brother in Massachusetts may still be shoveling snow, but here in the Northwest, it has been getting warmer, and things are changing. You can see the buds on the trees, but the best sign of spring is more rowers on the water. There are more women and men getting involved in the masters rowing groups, and the Everett Rowing Association's junior rowing teams, girls and boys from the high schools, are beginning practice for this year's competitions. However, the final guarantee that it is spring will be found on the river.

Once *Piper* is ready to launch, I take a trip to the dock with my oars and water bottle. Upon arrival, I see one of those signs of spring, a pair of mallards standing there. They won't be in my way, so I invite them to stay, but their better sense tells them to keep their distance from humans, and they give me a quack and fly off a short distance. I go back to the boathouse, lift *Piper* to my shoulders, carry her down to the dock, and launch.

I notice that the current is quite strong. There are only intermittent clouds in the sky now, but there has been a lot of rain in the last few days, and the warmer temperatures in the mountains have added lots of melted snow to the river flow. That is going to really slow my progress upstream. But these heavy currents are going to affect my travel in other ways as well. The large amount of water rushing through the river channel causes eddies that swirl this way and that as it flows. I can see the trail left by my boat wash back and forth as I row. Often, I feel the whole boat jerk to one side and then the other as I row through the stronger eddies. I keep my body loose and shift my weight as needed to be sure to keep balanced. I also keep a tight hand on the oars and take shorter strokes to be sure I can grab a hold of the water on one side if I start to fall over toward the other side.

There is less current in Steamboat Slough than in the main river, and the ride gets much smoother as I make the turn and head down. I can't help but notice the activity of the birds. They know it's spring. I see three mergansers swimming along by the riverbank, one female with two male companions. Further on I see two eagles perched on the limb of a high tree. For a while I have only been seeing them alone. Something is definitely going on these days. Here comes a pair of Canada geese flying toward me from downriver, honking as they pass overhead.

It has been light for some time, but the sun has just begun to rise over the mountains to the east. Still behind the trees as I row along the river, it becomes fully exposed in between gray, orange, and yellow clouds as I pass an opening between the trees. I make it to Turnaround Tree, turn around, and head home The sun is now above the trees, now shining on the still-bare limbs of the red and white alder trees and the occasional birch trees that grow on the west bank of the slough. Leaf buds have just begun to appear.

There are many species of birds around this time of year, and on this row, I am enjoying watching them fly overhead. There are always seagulls around, gliding whenever possible, with a very controlled stroking of their wings as needed to stay aloft. There are also lots of ducks. In contrast to the seagulls, ducks have to work harder to stay aloft, frantically flapping their wings as they speed across the river behind me. Particularly noticeable are the mergansers; unlike other ducks, they always fly low along the water. Of the birds I see on the river, the heron is the most unique in its flight. Its long neck, a valuable tool for catching fish, must be a problem in the air, but the heron makes it work by folding that neck in a tight S shape, becoming as graceful in flight as any bird. It is not always possible to tell which kind of a bird I am looking at. Right now I am looking at two large birds fly across the river behind me and land in a tree together. I can't tell what they are; all I could see was their dark shapes against the sky as they flew. I can tell by their shape that they aren't eagles; I think they are hawks of some kind, maybe a pair of ospreys.

Reaching the main river, I turn for home and find the current still strong and having its effects on the path of my boat. I almost row into a lone Canada goose. It squawks and flies a short distance, lands, and swims around idly, clearly irritated by my interruption. I am guessing that it is standing by a partner who is sitting on a nest somewhere nearby. Over there I see two eagles, each sitting on an old piling along the side of the river. One calls out and then flies over to join the other. They sit there chest to chest, each looking out in a different direction as if the other didn't exist.

Two Eagles on a Dolphin

Behind me on the river are the junior boys crews, two eights and a quad. I start pulling harder to test myself but am quickly passed. It is inspiring to see the coordinated strength of these boys producing such power as the boats speed by. I am sure those eagles were enjoying the show as well. The prize for being first back to the dock is to be able to pull out first. I have to wait a bit, but the boys work very quickly, and it doesn't take long before I have *Piper* up on her racks, and I am done for the day.

~

It is a Friday, and daylight savings time has arrived since my last row, robbing me of an hour of sleep and making sunrise later by the clock. The forecast is ideal, and looking out my window at the new 5:00 a.m., I see the sky full of stars. The weather is too perfect not to go for a row before heading for that office chair. As I drive to the boathouse, the dark shapes of the mountains against the very first light give me a preview of the row to come. It is still quite dark when I get to the boathouse, and the Morning Glories rowing group, locked into its hour on clock time, has again lost its daylight and is back on their rowing machines.

I ready *Piper* in the very early light and head down the ramp. A clear sky overnight has allowed the earth's heat to radiate away, and there is frost on the dock, and caution is required. The launch goes smoothly, and I head upriver. The sky is clear but for a few thin clouds; the rising sun gives them a rose-colored tint, which is mirrored in the calm water. As the sun rises, brightening up the sky, the color of the clouds turns to orange.

Morning Reflections on a Calm River

As I make the turn into the slough, I see Mount Olympus and the rest of the Olympic range bathed orange in the sun. The slough bends this way and that, and there is just a short distance where Mount Rainier briefly appears, only to be lost as I round the next turn.

Mount Rainier from Steamboat Slough

I see something leave the west bank and start swimming across the water. I had seen that same thing in about the same place last week; this must be near its home. It is not a bird, and it's not behaving like a seal. I slow down, hoping to find out what it is. Suddenly it rises out of the water and slaps its tail and dives out of sight; it's a beaver. Rowing on, I pass Eagle Tree and see just one eagle, whereas for a couple of trips I had been seeing two. I bet this guy is standing watch for a partner sitting in a nest somewhere nearby.

I row to Turnaround Tree and head home. It's a low tide, and I can see exposed along the bank the gnarled roots of the trees that line the slough. Above, I can see that those buds I have been seeing on the trees have begun to blossom into leaves. My passing disturbs a pair of mergansers. The trios and quartets I have been seeing on earlier rows seem now to have divided themselves into matched pairs. Instead of flying way off down the river, this pair just flies a short distance. I bet there is a nest not far off. A little further along, I encounter a pair of Canada geese; they, too, don't go far and must also have a nest that needs protecting.

Tree Roots Exposed at Low Tide

Rowing for home in the main river, I have Mount Rainier in view behind me just off to the west now in bright sunlight with Mount Baker in my forward-view mirror in the front. It is still calm, and the river reflects the bright blue sky. There is still frost on the float when I land. I see the footprints I left during my launch. But I also see that I haven't been the only one using the float in the predawn. There are the unmistakable three large toes of a heron. Walking up the ramp, I see that the large white alder tree at the head of the ramp is beginning to show its new leaves. Today was a true visual highlight.

~

"Clear with just a chance of morning fog in the a.m." is the forecast. For where I row, that chance is usually quite high. For the Morning Glories, that usually means another day on the rowing machines because it would be impossible for their coach to keep everyone in view. I am going out if I can see the trees on the other side of the river, and I will keep going as long as I can see both sides of the river. That is a very high tolerance and, although I have sometimes decided from home not to go because of the fog, I don't think I have ever turned back once I was on the water.

My test is passed, and I am off. I always know where I am, but with the limited visibility, I find myself straying over to one side of the river. I correct my course but before long find myself having strayed over to the other side. I am going to experience that several times again throughout the row. My forward-view mirror is fogging up, and it is not long before I have to stop and wipe it clear with the handkerchief I have folded up in my sock for just that purpose. I will be repeating that several times during this row.

At first light I could see fairly well through the fog, but now the sun is higher, and its reflection on the fog droplets has made the fog seem denser, and the visibility is worse. I can still see both sides of the river, and I still know where I am, but I do need to wipe off the mirror again to be sure that there isn't a log with my name on it or, worse, other rowers heading my way. It is still calm, and the trees along the bank are reflected in the water against the backdrop of the fog. It is too foggy to see the sun, but in the neighborhood where it should be, its rays illuminate the fog with a faint glow.

Naked Trees on a Calm, Foggy Morning

It was quite cool when I started, but it has warmed a bit, and I have generated some heat with my exercise. I am feeling a little overheated, and I need to remove a layer of clothing, not an easy job. The change of attire is going to take two hands, those same two hands I use to hold on to the oars to keep the boat from tipping over. To accomplish this feat, I press my chest up against the two oars, hoping that will keep them steady while I take off my windbreaker, remove the down vest, and then replace the windbreaker. With my two arms behind my back, one hand pulling the windbreaker sleeve off of the other arm, I feel particularly vulnerable. If one of those oars gets loose, I'll end up swimming. Success—this time at least. Whew!

Whak, whak, whak. The fog has brought me up unexpectedly on twelve Canada geese that were casually swimming in the river. Clearly irritated by the interruption, they nevertheless move over and let me by. With visibility restricted, there isn't much other wildlife to be seen on this trip. I concentrate on my rowing and where I am going, and I am soon back to the dock. I land and carry *Piper* up to the boathouse. The Midmorning masters rowing group has their boats ready to launch but is waiting for the fog to lift just a bit more. While I clean up and put *Piper* onto her rack, the fog lifts some more, and as I head to my car, I see the Midmorning rowers heading out.

The one thing I did see when I was rowing was that the skunk cabbages with their big leaves and bright yellow blossoms have begun to appear. This is the sign for me to take *Piper* to the garage for use in some open-water expeditions and replace her at the boathouse with *Molly*, a boat I named after the girl-child I never had. She is named *Molly*, the name I had proposed for the girl child we never had.

Molly

~

There is snow forecast for the east coast, but the TV meteorologist here has been promising a few nice days with temperatures into the seventies, and I hope to get out a couple of times this week. The morning twilight is early enough so that I can get on the water at about 6:00 a.m. As I carry my boat to the water, I see the Morning Glories readying their boats. This is my first time out on *Molly* this year. She is definitely faster than *Piper*, but the extra length and slimmer hull that makes for that extra speed make the boat more tender. It is taking me a while to get used to it again.

It is still a little chilly as I start out in the predawn twilight, but it is not long before my exercise makes me comfortable. The water is calm, and the sky is hazy but clear, a beautiful morning to be on the water. The leaves on the deciduous trees are more prominent; the lighter green of their new leaves stands out in contrast to the branches of their neighboring evergreens. The shrubs and vines along the banks that were brown all winter long, have also turned green with new growth. There is also a number of flowering trees along the river now in full bloom.

I see another creature working along the edge of the river and pause to watch. When it sees me, it slaps its tail and dives out of sight. I am guessing that it is the same beaver I saw the other day. A little further, I see two other creatures swimming along, one next to the bank to my left and the other fairly far away on the other side of the river. They are not acting like seals; they could be otters, but it is most likely that they are some other beavers. They both slip quietly out of sight, leaving me guessing.

I started out at just about high tide, and there was almost no current as I began my row. A little ways out, I cross a wave line across the river, the beginnings of the downstream current. Down the slough I can see a two-inch wet line on the trees along the bank, confirming the change. There will most certainly be a good current helping me along when I get back to the main river. While I was out, the Morning Glories launched and went for their row. As I reach the main river, I see them on the water, three quads, two rowed by women and one by men, and a couple of singles. It is a pleasure to see other rowers on the river.

There are a series of tall light poles along the west side of the main river. There has always been a lot of bird activity on these poles, and recently I had seen a new collection of branches at the top of one of them. As I row by today, I can see its purpose. There is the white head of an eagle appearing above the branches of this nest. On the next pole over sits another eagle keeping watch. As the seasons progress, it is going to be fun to see the family develop.

Eagle Nest on a Light Pole

A couple of years ago on another light pole further upriver, I got to watch a couple of ospreys raise their young. Like the eagles today, one of the couple sat on the nest while the mate watched from nearby. During the summer, I could see the two offspring in the nest and watch them grow. By fall, they were gone. Last year, there seemed to be a dispute between the ospreys and the eagles. I saw a number of eagles, but my only memory of an osprey that year was seeing one fly across the river with a large stick in its beak for a nest somewhere away from this part of the river. I can still see the uninhabited remains of the osprey nest. It looks like this year it's eagle territory.

It's not far from the eagle's nest to the dock. As I land, I see two seals playing together in the middle of the river. A few moments later, as I get ready to lift *Molly* out of the water, I see a big swirl in the water a short way off. The two seals surface, give me a quick glance, and swim away. As I walk up the ramp, I see two Canada geese sitting on one of the breakwater logs, talking to each other. At the top of the ramp, I glance as always at the big white alder tree across the road, its leaves now in full bloom. I clean up and head to work.

Welcoming Alder in Spring

~

It is another one of those days when the forecast isn't too friendly: showers with increasing wind. However, I have been having some good luck these days staying out from under the showers. The wind doesn't look too deadly, and I might be able to avoid it if I get on the water early. Driving to the boathouse, I see some dark clouds, but it isn't raining, and the breeze right now looks manageable. It's not like I am going to be out in open water; being down on the water below the riverbanks protects me from the full force of the wind, and the curving path of the river prevents any large buildup of waves.

I launch and head up the river. I haven't gone too far when I see a large black cloud moving from west to east behind me. It is quite a distance off, and it looks fairly well self-contained. I think it is going to be best for me to keep upriver of it. It is moving fairly fast and will probably be gone by the time I return to the dock. Oh, I see a couple of lightning strikes come from the cloud; I am definitely going to stay upriver.

Watch Out—There Is a Storm Coming

The wind is against me on the river, but it is heading in the same direction as the current, so the waves it is generating aren't getting too large. It is necessary to lift the oars a little further out of the water on the recovery to get them above the waves. That doesn't always succeed; every now and again the oar hits a wave, tilting the boat just slightly to the other side. It's still manageable, but it does make me recall why I enjoy rowing on calm water. Waves don't usually get as large on Steamboat Slough, so I turn and take my usual route.

It's becoming clear that I didn't beat the wind; it has been getting stronger and stronger. With the many turns of the slough, the waves are not getting too big, but it is definitely having its effect on my boat speed. As I'm heading down the slough, the wind is now behind me, adding measurably to my speed. The greater density of the wavelets caused by an increase in the wind makes the water darker under a gust; I can see these *cat's paws* move toward me across the water and feel the added pressure of the wind on my body and its effect on the boat when it hits. I am happy to see that the black cloud has moved on. The sky now is covered with the dramatic hills and valleys on the underside of the clouds in their varying shades of grays.

Down a ways, Steamboat Slough does straighten out in a direction parallel with the wind, allowing some significant waves to build. It might have been best to turn around early, but I challenge myself and row all the way to Turnaround Tree, now feeling the slap of the oars on the waves and the consequent rolling of the boat back and forth. Arriving at my objective, I turn and head back. Until I get to the main river, the wind and waves will be against me. I give up my thoughts of a smooth and fast row and settle down to what is just the work ahead for me.

I finally make it to the main river. I can see that the waves have gotten larger than they were when I rowed up. I pause for a minute or two to catch my breath and ready myself for the final dash home. Now I am off. The wind is behind me, and the boat is now sort of surfing down the waves. I say "sort of" because the waves aren't pushing me straight ahead but rather first off to one side and then off to the other. It's best to take short strokes and keep the oars high on the recovery. I pass a man walking the river trail. I hear him yell, "Are you crazy?" I wished I had that excuse. I feel somewhat secure in the knowledge that both the wind and current are in my favor and that even if I just sat there, not rowing at all, focused solely on keeping my balance, I would still eventually get back to the dock. It is also just a short swim to the nearest shore. However, I am able to keep up a steady stroke rate, and these waves are still nothing compared to what they would be in open water.

A large flock of birds high in the sky, probably Canada geese, is being affected by the wind as well. A gust of wind hits them, distorting their formation. The birds stay in their lines, but the lines are now bent up and down and off to the left and right. As the birds work to get back into formation, another gust arrives, creating additional distortions. The formation now has the look of abstract art. When the gust passes the geese adjust their flight to move back into their V formation.

I need to get back. I reach the dock and pull *Molly* out of the water. Heading up the ramp, the wind pushes on the boat, and I struggle to keep it straight. I manage to get it onto the slings, dried off, and onto its rack in the boathouse. This has been one of those rows that I am feeling better about now that it's done. Well, it didn't rain.

∼

It's going to be one of those special spring days: clear, calm, and northwest warm once the sun gets up. A day like this can bring extra joy to a row. The morning twilight makes its appearance early this time of year, and I have set an early alarm to try to beat the sun to the boathouse. I will arrive at 5:15 a.m. and will be able to get on the water a full two hours earlier than was possible in January. The Morning Glories row this morning, but they won't arrive for quite a while.

As I carry *Molly* down the ramp, I see two Canada geese pacing around in the now quite tall river grass; between them in constant motion are four babies, the first sign of new life I have seen this year. The sun isn't visible yet, but as I seat myself on the sliding seat and insert my feet into the foot stretchers, I see through the haze that it has risen far enough to illuminate Mount Baker in pink far to the north. I dig my outboard oar into the water to catch the current that will pull me away from the dock and out into the river.

A Calm Start, Mount Baker in the Distance

It is completely calm, and the blue sky and the few light clouds are perfectly matched in the reflection on the river, distorted only by the splash of my oars and the light wake of the boat. I row over to the west side of the river to check on the eagles. I can see the white head of one eagle sticking out from the nest high on the light pole with the mate sitting guard on another pole nearby. Further on, as I row past the old osprey nest, I am surprised to see a bird fly in with a branch. I was wrong; the ospreys did come back. I guess the two species have reached an understanding; it will be nice to see how they coexist to raise their respective families.

It is still calm when I turn down Steamboat Slough. The sun is fully up and following me from the other side of the trees along the riverbank. There are occasional patches of a light river fog, but the visibility is not affected. The vegetation along the banks is now fully green, and the wild roses are in bloom. It looks like there is snow on the river. The alder trees have released their cottony seed pods, and they are collected into small patches all over the river.

I hear a splash from up ahead and off to my right. It is no doubt one of the river critters irritated by my interruption. One of the disadvantages of rowing is only getting to look ahead in the occasional glance into the forward-view mirror. The seals never seem to mind my presence, but the beavers and otters see me coming and, most of the time, manage to disappear just about the time I learn that they are there.

I can see in my mirror that I am coming up on a pair of Canada geese idly swimming along. As I near, one of them calmly swims off to the side. The other, spooked by my approach, squawks loudly and flies off a short distance. However, the bird has landed directly in my path, and I am quickly upon it. As I approach, again it squawks, again it flies a short distance, and again lands directly in my path. Another squawk, another takeoff, and another landing directly in my path. This drama repeats itself three or four times before the goose flies over to the side of the river out of my way, where it watches angrily as I row by.

I have rowed far enough; it is time to turn around and head back. The sun is now well above the trees, reflecting brilliantly in the calm water and making it a little difficult to see. I can see a heron up ahead sitting peacefully on an old piling on the side of the river. Unnerved by my approach, it flies off to a more secure location. Further along, I see four Canada geese near the riverbank swimming herd on a fleet of new babies.

As I turn down the river toward the dock, I meet the Morning Glories rowing group heading out. There are two quads, one men's and one women's, a man and woman in singles, and two women in a double. Their coach, shouting occasional instructions, keeps an eye on all from her launch, while her husky dogs watch the proceedings from the bow. It's good to see others enjoying this great physical experience on this beautiful river. There are others out enjoying the morning. Far off to the south, I see a colorful hot-air balloon rising high in the sky. Before long, I see a second.

I am soon back at the dock. As I hoist *Molly* overhead, a seal swims close by and gives me a curious eye. I walk up the ramp, greeted again by the alder tree up ahead. *Molly* goes on her rack, and I head to the office.

THIRTEEN

SUMMER

Summer has officially come. However, in the Northwest, reliable warm weather doesn't always arrive for a while. Right now there is a low-pressure cell centered just off the coast, bringing cooler than normal temperatures and waves of rain up from the south. The forecast is for a short period of relief tomorrow morning before a heavy rain front comes in. I lay out my rowing gear, get to bed early, rise at four, and leave the house at five. The sky is clear, and the mountains are out, but it is a little cooler than it should be for this time of year, and there is a little breeze, so I need an extra layer to be comfortable.

As I carry *Molly* down the ramp, I encounter several families of Canada geese—mothers, fathers, and their now fast-growing offspring—feeding in the river grasses along the shore. They don't appear to be disturbed at all by my arrival. I launch and head upriver against a strong current. This is my first row after attending a three-day session at the Craftsbury Sculling Center in upstate Vermont, and I am anxious to try to adopt the things I learned. They had much to tell me, but I came away focused on gliding longer between strokes and keeping the oars closer to the surface during the drive. The current is quite strong, and the swirling eddies that I encounter push the boat back and forth; it is important that I keep my upper body synchronized with the swaying of the boat to keep it stable. The current will be much calmer once I turn into Steamboat Slough, one of the reasons I like to row there.

My first destination is the eagles' nest. I haven't seen any birds around the nest for a couple of weeks now; I am afraid that something interrupted this eagle pair's efforts to raise their family and they have moved away. Rowing on, I see that a large barge has been parked along the shore, right under the osprey nest. It appears there are plans to load it with dirt. The ospreys aren't obviously present as they had been; I am afraid that the activity around the barge has caused them to move on as well. The eagles and ospreys are gone, but one of the nice things about summer is the presence of people walking along a trail along the east side of the river, frequently with their dogs and sometimes with kids on bikes or in strollers.

As I make the turn into the slough, an eagle flies right overhead and then soars out over the river, its white head and tail brightly lit by the sun. A little further on, I see another eagle perched awkwardly on a high tree branch, two crows flying around it, obviously irritated at its presence. These are the first two eagles I have seen in some time. Perhaps they are the two that abandoned that nest.

One of the first things you come to on the slough is a line of boats moored on a dock along the south shore, some work boats and some pleasure craft. Some of these serve as homes for their owners; others have just been placed there, I gather, because moorage is cheap. For some of these boats, this is the end of the line. Over the years, I have seen boats parked here until they sink. Some of these derelicts have been removed by the state department of ecology, but a number of others are still where they went down, monuments to their owners' disrespect for the value the boat had when it was useful and irresponsibility to that place in nature where they were left. Boats are just collections of wood, fiberglass, aluminum, and steel, but they are human creations and have been part of human activity since the very early days of our species.

Boats of some sort have been part of my life from my early childhood. It is sad to see these thoughtlessly abandoned. I will feel a little relieved when I get beyond them.

As I row into the more natural surroundings, I start to think about my Craftsbury lessons: glide more between each stroke and keep my hands low when I pull to keep the oars from digging too deep in the water. Since rowing is normally such an unthinking process for me, I have to keep reminding myself to concentrate on my lessons. My Speed Coach confirms that I am going faster with less exertion when I do it right.

The cattails along the banks are growing tall now. Occasionally among them I see a slender, red-leafed plant; it makes a nice contrast to all the green. I wish I knew what that plant was. The tweeting of the sparrows is almost constant, and just now I see two of them flying circles around each other. Over there in the dead branches of a tree is an osprey keeping watch. At another place on the river, I can hear but not see a woodpecker tapping away on a tree. Now again is that brief opportunity to see Mount Rainier, orange in the morning sun. This is going to be a good day to row around Otter Island.

Just before Ebey Slough joins Steamboat Slough, it branches into two streams, creating Otter Island. The Everett Rowing Association sponsors a row around the island every fall, followed by a big feast. Now on my own, I row up Ebey Slough for about a half of a mile to the entrance of the other stream. As I near the entrance to that other stream, my oar catches on the limb of a sunken tree I hadn't seen; the boat tips to the side. I grab for the water with my other oar and manage to avoid capsizing. Because the current is running strong, my timing has to be good to get safely into the narrow entrance to that other stream. It is definitely the smaller stream, and it gets shallow in places. A few years ago, I did this trip at near low tide and had to carry the boat for about a hundred feet over the muddy bottom. The tide isn't so low now, but I can see several deadheads sticking out of the water and one ripple in the water where another lurks just beneath the surface. My carefully chosen course gets me around all of these, and I make it back to the wider and deeper Steamboat Slough and head back to the dock. As I stop for a short rest, I can hear the soft coo of a morning dove.

I again focus on my Craftsbury lessons and am rowing smoothly. Behind me I see an eagle fly over the river and hover near the water, focused on a particular spot. It looks about to dive but changes its mind and flies up and lands in a tree. Rowing a little further, I hear a long, loud squawk. I never saw it, but I am guessing that it was a heron expressing its displeasure about something. I make it back to the main river and head for the dock. I can see Mount Rainier again, but this time, above it but off to the east a bit, there is a lenticular cloud, an isolated round cloud consisting of condensed water vapor in the air flowing up over the mountain. That forecast for the rain and clouds to swing around the low-pressure cell and hit us sometime today is probably correct. I head to the dock, put *Molly* away, and go home. The clouds did fill in, and although it never got windy like it does in winter or spring, it sure rained.

∼

Summer can be a good time for some extended rows. It's a beautiful day with white clouds in a blue sky. I decide to row around Ebey Island again, about a 15.3-mile trip along the land. The perfect time to row around Ebey Island occurs when a fading up-river current boosts you along until you reach the entrance to the Ebey Slough and then changes to a downriver current to get you back home. A look at the tide tables tells me that that is not going to happen for some time. Indeed, today it looks like I will be facing an outgoing king tide where an extra-high tide flows out to an extra-low minus tide, creating an extra-strong downstream current. However, if I am going to do an extended row, this is still the best choice, and I will at least get the benefit of a helpful current down the Ebey Slough.

It is Saturday, and there are a number of masters rowers at the boathouse. I get launched while they are organizing themselves and probably won't see them on the water; they will finish their row long before I am done. The swirling and fast-moving current holds my attention as I proceed up the main river, and I am constantly having to make small course corrections as I row. A comparison of the through-the-water distance on the Speed Coach and the along-the-land distance on the GPS tells me what kind of a current I am dealing with. I figure that my travel through the water is about a third further than my travel along the land.

I stay on the river, pass the turnoff to Steamboat Slough, and soon come to Everett's river waterfront. Once upon a time, it was busy here. It was the center for lots of boats carrying passengers and cargo up and down the river and onshore businesses dealing with the people and goods that arrived. These days, it appears that there is little commercial business this far up the river. There are boats, mostly used in the fishing industry, parked there permanently, unused docks, many abandoned buildings, and onshore piles of unknown materials. The area has a great potential for recreational uses, and Everett has plans in the works. Right now it's a little sad to see the area going to waste.

Passing under the Highway US 2 bridge, I soon come to an old derrick used by many rowers as a good place to turn around, but I am going on. On the east side of the river, there are farmlands. There are cows grazing along the riverbank; one or two of them look over at me as I pass. Over on the west side, there are endless rows of old moss-covered pilings with grass and an occasional small tree growing out of the top, put there long ago for purposes no longer known. I pass under the high-voltage power lines, three and a third miles along the land from where I launched but four and a half through the water. On the top of the tower on the west, I see my first eagle of the trip.

I reach the community of Lowell; now a part of Everett, it was once an independent port on the Snohomish River. The only signs today of the logging and other commerce that thrived there along the water are more of those pilings along the shore. The river makes a right-angle turn at Lowell, and I turn from southbound to eastbound to continue upriver.

In another mile along the land, I reach the entrance to Ebey Slough. There are several deadheads at the entrance and, once the turn is made, two pilings right in the middle of the channel. Careful navigation done with aid of my forward-view mirror gets me through, and I am on my way down the slough. To this point, I have rowed five and a half miles along the land and eight miles through the water. Happily, the current is now with me. Over there is another eagle sitting on another high-voltage power-line tower. Seen before during early-spring rows but now hidden in the leaves, there is an eagles' nest that has been active for a number of years.

The Ebey Slough flows first through farmland. I can't see much from my vantage point on the water below the riverbanks, but the trees are mostly gone, and I can see the tops of a couple of barns as I row by. The upper part of the Ebey Slough winds back and forth, and I find that I have to pull hard with one oar or the other to stay in the channel. Every now and again I realize that I have returned to my old habits and am not using the form I learned at Craftsbury. It is going to be important to remind myself to think about it every now and again until it becomes habitual. My passage along the land is going much faster with the current in my favor, and it's not long before trees close in along both banks of the river.

Highway US 2 passes over Ebey Slough on two low bridges. I slow down to carefully aim for a path between their cement pilings. As I begin to pass under the bridge, hundreds of swallows fly into the air, circling around and around in all directions. Looking up underneath the bridge, I see their mud nests, and I row along, hoping not to disturb the birds any more than I already have.

Not far along on the west side of the slough is another one of those riverside marinas with a number of old boats that have been there a long time and are not likely to go to sea again. Passing on, I row back into farmlands. From my vantage point on the water, I can't see much right on the other side of the levee, but on the hill beyond, I can see homes on the outskirts of the town of Lake Stevens. At about twelve miles of my trip along the land, I reach the junction of the Ebey and Steamboat Sloughs. The current has been with me since leaving the main river. Nevertheless, on the trip as a whole, I have spent more of my time working against the current, and I have still rowed through the water a couple of additional miles, and it's time for a rest. With the noise of my rowing silenced, I can hear the swallows chirping and the tapping of a woodpecker. It's nice to be able to just sit here and not move and enjoy the scenery.

Rowing where I do is a little like driving on a road through a pretty countryside. The difference, of course, is that the path I am on is water, which reflects the trees and plants along the sides of the river and the sky in its center. These reflections are really sharp on the calm waters of an early morning. As I take a stroke and start *Molly* moving again, I feel encouraged in my venture by the fluffy white clouds in the bright blue sky above reflected clearly in the water I am rowing on.

It's about three miles along the land back to the dock. The current is against me in Steamboat Slough, but once in the main river, it helps me finish swiftly. When I get back to the dock, my GPS tells me that I have traveled 15.77 miles along the land, and my Speed Coach shows that I rowed 17.62 miles through the water. I'm going home and take it really easy for the rest of the day.

~

It is another beautiful morning, a little light north breeze, but it's warm, and the sky is clear. This is a good day to row around Smith and Spencer Islands. I start a little later than usual, but there are a number of groups going out, and I want to stay out of their way. The sun has long been up, but I can see a faint full moon just setting in the west. My trip starts downriver. It's a little after high tide, and there is a strong current helping me along. I soon see the Morning Glories rowing group in two quads rowing upstream, and I head over to the side to let them pass.

Just as it is upriver, there are many pilings with no current purpose, but unlike upstream, there are also a number of active businesses along the shore. This part of Everett retains its historic focus on muscle and big machines doing heavy work, leaving all that tech work for Seattle and points south. On the west side of the river is a large railroad yard where railcars carrying oil, coal, or cargo containers are being assembled and where the occasional passenger train speeds through. The first thing I come to on the east side is Dagmars Marina. Boats there are kept on land and placed in the water at the request of their owners. There are a number of boats sitting at the dock, waiting for their owners to take them out on this beautiful day. Passing on, I come to a large barge being fed woodchips for a pulp mill and then a yard where logs are collected for transport to a sawmill.

In close succession, I pass under the highway bridge for State Route 529 and the railroad bridge that parallels it. Both are old through-truss bridges supported by networks of iron girders; the highway bridge draws open, and the railroad bridge pivots around for large boat traffic, not a problem for me. Once through there, the river widens out as it arrives at Port Gardner Bay, and I start looking for my course to the east. It gets very shallow here, and it is a good thing I'm here near high tide; I have run aground here on other trips.

Turning the point, I enter a large bay with pilings everywhere, some in rows a regular distance apart and others side by side as a breakwater. The human purpose long since over, they now provide perching and nesting for waterfowl. I see occupied osprey nests on two of the pilings, others providing seagulls and other birds with a place to rest. There are also quite a few cormorants standing on the pilings, many with their wings outstretched, drying in the sun, an image apparently used by John Milton in *Paradise Lost* to represent Satan. Cruising through the water are lots of seals; over there is a mother with her young pup. Far behind me through the summer haze, I can see the Olympic Mountains with their snow all but gone.

Cormorants on Pilings

I am never completely sure where to head until I see the derrick and dry dock of the boatyard on the west side of the entrance to the Steamboat Slough. The course adjusted, and a hundred more strokes bring me to another railroad bridge passing low over the river. I don't have to actually duck to get through, but the often-painted and now rusty span is right in my face as I clear. Three hundred feet further, I pass under the separate spans for the east and west travel on Highway SR 529 and in a couple of hundred yards more, under the high bridge for Interstate 5.

Now I am back in the more natural surroundings of Steamboat Slough with several miles of strong currents to fight. It is a long way, but all the navigational challenges have been met, and I let my mind drift off with only occasional interruptions to check on my rowing form. There is not much to see right here, a barn and farmhouse on the west side and a swampy area on the east—time to just row. It's about two miles to Turnaround Tree, my usual turnaround spot when coming the other way, and another half mile to Eagle Tree, where I would turn around years ago. I am feeling strong and relaxed.

Up ahead, I see a number of junior rowers from the Everett Rowing Association resting and listening to instructions from their coach from his outboard launch. There are a couple of doubles and a number of single sculls. I get by and a couple hundred yards ahead when they start coming in my direction. I start to row faster, but it soon becomes clear that these juniors are going to catch and pass me with ease. I console myself by remembering that I have rowed eight miles by this point, but on consideration I conclude it's the youth, energy, and training that take them past me and away. What a good time for a drink of water and a short rest.

From here, it's just looking like work. I am tired, and it's getting hot. I find some inspiration by focusing on the form of my stroke. Looking around, it's also encouraging to see a heron standing patiently on a piling on the side of the river and, a little later, to have another give me a loud squawk as it flies across the river behind me. Further along, I see a flock of Canada geese flying high overhead. I am imagining that a lot of these are this year's newborns being conditioned by their parents for their flight south this winter.

With my energies renewed, I finish the last mile against the current in Steamboat Slough and then turn down-current in the main river to finish my row to the dock. Those juniors I encountered earlier have their boats put away by the time I get my boat up from the water and are receiving an encouraging talk from their coach as I clean up and put *Molly* on her racks. It's time now to go home and get out of the heat.

∼

The days of summer are marching along, and I have been wanting to take the extra time to row around Jetty Island. Jetty Island is a long, thin, sandy island at the end of the Snohomish River that runs between two and three 1000 feet off the shore along much of the Port of Everett. It's a city park, and people go there to enjoy the sandy beaches and observe the birds that make it their home.

Arriving at the boathouse, I notice that the tide is quite low and, in talking to one of the other rowers, am reminded how shallow it is, particularly around the east end of Jetty Island. However, the tide is coming in and would take me a while to get there, so I am going to go see what I find. I put *Molly* into the water and head out, passing around some of the Morning Glory rowers that launched just ahead of me.

Not far along, I pass close to an osprey perched in its nest on some pilings with its partner on another piling not far away. As I continue, I notice a number of other ospreys at work and a number of cormorants standing on pilings with their wings outstretched to dry. The sun is well up to the east with the mountains appearing below it as dark shapes against the blue sky. There is activity at the businesses along the river, but I am paying more attention to the state of the tides and worrying that I may be rowing into trouble.

Osprey on Nest, Partner Standing By

The river empties into the bay at the east end of Jetty Island, and I decide to try going around that end first and row around the island counterclockwise to learn early whether this expedition is going to work at all. The water is shallow, and I can see the bottom, but so far I am still floating. I can feel myself going slower in the shallows. The wave made by a boat moving through the water is more than a ripple above the surface; it's also a movement of water down under the boat. When that part of the wave comes against the bottom, it forces the energy back up, and the boat slows down. This is something a rower can really feel because it becomes harder to pull the oars through the water.

Uh-oh, the skeg has started dragging through the sand, but maybe it's only for a short distance…no, I am stuck. I can't make it through and have to turn back. The boat is still floating, barely; it's the skeg that is stuck. I take off my footwear, climb out, turn the boat around, and wade back the way I came for a hundred yards or so, pulling *Molly* behind. I think it's deep enough now, and I climb back in and start rowing again. There is deeper water along the south side of Jetty Island, and I decide to at least row down to the west end.

Jetty Island began as a breakwater of rocks built in the late 1800s to provide some protection to Everett Harbor. Material dredged out of the Snohomish River has been placed there, and over the years the river itself has contributed silt it washed down from the mountains. The original wall of rocks is now mostly covered with sand that is now populated in places with shrubs and the occasional tree. A sandy beach surrounds the island, which is particularly evident during this low tide. Across on the mainland, I row past some industries; a shallow expanse with rows of pilings where logs are stored, far less now than in the past; a boat launch; a large marina for fishing boats and pleasure craft; some waterfront restaurants; and the Everett Naval Station. The trip along this side of the island is being slowed by the incoming tidal current, but I have made it to the end and have to decide what to do now.

If I try to continue around, I could run aground again. However, it's calm, and waters of the whole bay reflect the light blue of the sky; it will be nice to row out there even if I have to retreat and travel back the way I came. Besides, the tide is coming in and may increase the depth enough over the sandbar by the time I get there. So, I am going to try it.

As I start out, a seagull sees me while flying by, sets his course for mine, comes right up behind, and when right overhead, veers off in a new direction. Meanwhile, on the sandy beach of the island sits a large flock of its fellow seagulls, squawking loudly to one another. Even a hundred feet from shore, although deep enough for me, it's still very shallow. I see an object sticking out of the water ahead covered with barnacles. A little closer, I realize I am passing over the remains of a wrecked ship and have to change course to avoid the chance of running into part of the structure hiding just below the surface. Out in the bay, I stop to watch a large swarm of small seabirds flying around and around, this way and that, in no set pattern but always in perfect coordination.

Jetty Island is a popular launch site for kite surfers, and I recall dining at one of those waterfront restaurants and enjoying seeing glimpses of the kites flying through the sky with the surfers speeding across the waters of the bay below. Fortunately for me in my much slower trip, it is still almost completely calm. The rowing is easier without the waves, and the blue reflection of the sky provides a peaceful setting for my efforts.

I am nearing the area where I had to turn around, and it is encouraging to see that the sandbar that extended out into the bay here on the east end of the island isn't as prominent as it was. I can see the sandy bottom not far below, and the boat is slowing down from the shallows, but I only need to get a little further to be where it was deep enough before. My starboard oar hits the sand but still manages to pull through. Just a couple more strokes—one, two, three…whew, I made it to where I know it's deep enough.

The rest of the trip will be easier. It's not too far, and I am aided by the upstream current of the still-flooding tide. I pass two shells from the Midmorning Rowing Group heading out. It is not long before I land at the dock, put *Molly* away, and head home.

FOURTEEN

Fall

The calendar tells me it's fall. But there have been other signs as well. We just had our first big fall rain, and our time with the sun is getting shorter at a rate of more than three minutes a day. Because my time is flexible, I can start my row a little later, now after the start of the Morning Glories' session. We are going to hit the water at about the same time because the darkness has kept them on rowing machines for the first part of their session. The sky was clear when I left the house, but as I approach the clubhouse, I encounter a third sign that it is fall: return of fog on the river. It's a light fog but a clear sign of what's to come. Once the Morning Glory rowers have shoved off, I take *Molly* down to the dock and shove off too.

The River on a Calm Morning

Over to my left—remember I am facing backward—is a railroad engine being hooked up to its hundreds of freight cars. They are almost always there, and I have come not to give them much thought until, as now, I hear the *bang, bang, bang, bang* as each car is jerked into motion. The railroad runs right along the river for a ways. I am moving faster than the train as it starts, but I can see it picking up speed and gaining on me as it heads off where the tracks and river separate.

I am just going to do my usual row up the river, down Steamboat Slough, to Turnaround Tree, and return. It is a little cooler these days, so I am glad I am wearing my windbreaker. It occurs to me that this is just the first step to late-fall and winter rowing, when it will be much colder and I will be wearing more layers of heavier clothes. I am also thinking that I will have to challenge myself to get up in total darkness and hit the water at very first light. I tell myself not to be too negative; there will be some very nice rows here in the fall, and I will meet the challenges of winter when they come.

The river is in the last stages of a flooding tide, and I get a little assistance rowing up the river. The numbers on the Speed Coach are not what I would like; I am going a third of a mile slower than I have been. Well, I have been on holiday, away from the river for three weeks and eating too freely. The extra weight sinks the boat deeper into the water, and the loss of muscle tone is making it harder than usual to move the extra water aside.

As I row down Steamboat Slough, I can see that the leaves on the red alder trees are beginning to turn. Northwest foliage in the fall is nothing like the beautiful fall foliage in the New England. The native trees of this area just turn at best to a sad kind of yellow and then brown, or they just shrivel and fall. That's too bad, but I console myself with the thought that I will find days in winter to get out on the water when my northeastern counterparts are finding only ice on the water. The Northwest trees in the fall may be disappointing, but I can see reds, yellows, oranges, and purples against the fading green in the bushes along the bank. I can also pick out the wild roses, now with their plump, reddish-orange seed pods. The cattails, too, are quite striking with their fully mature brown seed heads standing high over the now-wilting leaves. The ubiquitous green of summer has been replaced for just a while with a diversity of color.

My attention turns inward and interspersed with thoughts about the troubles of the world, I concentrate on trying to get my speed back: stretching further back on the recovery for a longer hold on the water during the drive, keeping the oars shallow, timing the hardest exertion for the point where the oars have the greatest leverage, and remembering to let the boat glide to get the full effect of that exertion. These things do seem to bring back some of the speed I had lost. I make it to Turnaround Tree, turn around, and head back.

It's mostly just work from here, but in time, I am back. The Morning Glories had finished their row and have left the boathouse, but the Midmorning Group is bringing their oars down to the dock as I arrive. I put *Molly* away and head off to the office. I am finishing a lot later than I was in late spring and summer, and I don't have time to go home to clean up. Starting today, I will be showering at work.

∼

In contrast to my last time out, today looks like a perfect day for a row. Invasions by low-pressure fronts with their clouds and showers are becoming more and more common, but we often get a nice day or sometimes just a part of a nice day in between. When I arrive at the boathouse, the sun is out, and it's calm. The tide is way out, and it is a long way down the ramp to the dock. Hopefully, the tide will have come in some by the time I return so that I won't have too steep a climb up the ramp. I launch *Molly* and head upriver. There is still just a bit of downstream current to contend with.

The low tide has exposed a sandy beach along the west side of the river. There are two separate groups of Canada geese encamped there, no doubt making preparations for their winter trip south. It's good to see these geese again before they leave. It's Sunday, and I am probably going to be the only rower on the river, but across the river from the geese, there are a number of people walking on the trail, enjoying the nice weather.

Turning down Steamboat Slough, I startle two mergansers, the first I've seen this season, and they fly off down the river, low over the water in typical merganser fashion. A little further on, I see a kingfisher fly off its perch on a low-hanging limb over the water, complaining that I have disturbed its fishing; that action is repeated by a second one a little further on. Probably because of the fog on my last row, I didn't see a single animal; it's good to see more action this time. There is a heron looking elegant over on the side of the river. Herons are the one large bird that stays around through the summer; I have been consistently sighting them flying across the river or perched along the bank, patiently waiting for a fish to swim near.

As I pass Eagle Tree on the way out, I see an eagle sitting in the sun on a high branch. This is the first eagle I have seen in over a month. It's my guess that the eagles have been away someplace where the salmon are plentiful. Maybe this guy is scouting the Snohomish and its tributaries to see if the salmon are back here yet. I had heard that they had opened fishing on the river for a couple of days on a couple of weekends because more Coho salmon were returning than had been expected. I have been expecting to see fishermen on the river, and seeing this eagle, I am now hoping what will attract the fishermen will bring back more eagles as the fall carries on.

In the last half mile before my turnaround, I encounter two deadheads that must have floated in since my last row. Some recent extra-high tides lifted them from where they were, and the strong accompanying currents placed them in their new locations, one right in mid channel. Avoiding these hazards, I reach Turnaround Tree and head back. It is easy to let a new obstacle drop from one's thoughts, particularly on the row home. I keep myself alert, manage with the help of my forward-view mirror to navigate around the two new deadheads, and then fall back into my almost automatic adjustments to those obstacles that have been in place for a while. As I pass Eagle Tree, I don't see the eagle that was there on my way down, but as I row on, it flies back in to take its place again on the same branch of the same tree.

A little breeze has come up during my time on the slough, and I have been noticing the varying effects of it and the current on my boat speed. The slowing effect of the head wind on my speed through the water was made worse when I was rowing with the current down the slough. On my return against the current, the wind helping me through the water feels stronger than it actually is. When I get into the river where the wind and current are running in the same direction, the wind will not affect my speed through the water as much.

I put my focus on rowing and am soon at the head of Steamboat Slough and turn down the main river toward the dock. I am not surprised to see that, indeed, a number of outboard boats of various sizes have launched and are fishing on the river. With the help of my forward-view mirror, I am able to stay out of their way and make it back to the dock. The fishermen will be partners on the river for a while. I land, shoulder *Molly*, and head up the ramp. I can't help noticing that in contrast to the red alders, the leaves on that white alder that always welcomes me home at the top of the ramp still have a few more days in their summer green. There is fog on the river again. The earth has radiated away its heat into the clear night sky, cooling the water vapor rising from the river and condensing it to fog. It is much foggier than it was the other day, but the water is calm, and as I bring *Molly* down to the dock, I can still see the other side of the river even now in the predawn light. It is quite cold—in the thirties—and I am wearing long pants and three upper layers for the first time this fall. I think this may be my last trip on the river in *Molly*. The tide is quite low and still going down, and I walk cautiously down the ramp; it is quite dark, and I want to avoid slipping on the frost that I am guessing might have formed. All goes well, and I launch and am away. Oh, there is another sign of the season: my fingers are tingling with the cold.

It is still fairly dark when I make the turn down Steamboat Slough. Officially the sun has risen, and I can see it reflecting through the fog on the windows of some buildings across the river. However, it won't get over the Cascade Mountains far enough to light up the river area for a while. As I row down the slough, I see through the fog the dark contorted shapes of the roots and stumps exposed along the banks by the low tide. It is quiet except for my breathing and the sound of my oars, and it feels a bit gloomy and mysterious. They are hard to make out, but there is a heron on the bank to my left and, a little further, another on a piling over on my right; both silently observe me pass.

The fog is dense but fairly shallow; I can see the sky above. There are scattered thin clouds in the blue sky, now orange in this stage of the sun's rise. As I row down the slough the sun rises more and those clouds turn white. The sun itself isn't yet visible, but I can now see it lighting up the tops of the trees. As I near my turnaround, I start to see its bright light in the fog behind the trees. It's not long before I begin to see the edge of the sun itself, and shortly after, the whole sun is visible.

Reaching Turnaround Tree, I head back. It's still foggy, and the lowering tide has me even deeper in the river channel, but the sunshine has fully invaded the scene, and given me more energy to put into my rowing. The herons I pass on the return—maybe the same ones I saw going out, maybe not—seem more animated as well. One of them manages to stay put as I pass, but the other flies off. I concentrate on my rowing, trying to keep my speed through the water over seven miles an hour. That brings me to the mouth of the slough, and I head downriver to the dock.

The sun has begun to warm up the air, and there is much less fog in the main river. The current helps me home, and it's not long before I row under the I-5 bridge. I do have to pull over to the side of the river; a couple of quads, two doubles, and a single shell from the Midmorning rowing group are assembled, waiting for their coach to lead them on their day's outing. I land, lift *Molly* onto my shoulders, and head toward the boathouse. There is a little frost on the dock, and I am glad for my caution during launch. I put *Molly* away and go home.

~

Between outings, I have switched boats. I took *Molly* home and brought *Piper* down to my racks at the boathouse. Fall and winter weather brings more hazards to the river, and *Piper*'s greater stability and righting ability in the event of a capsize make her a good choice. I'm up early, eager to get out on the water on one of those few days without rain and wind that matches one of the opportunities on my calendar. Today, I am the only one at the boathouse. I had heard some gunfire yesterday, so I spend a few minutes before launching to again tape my air horn to the rigger so that I can let the hunters know that I am out there. The launch goes easily, and I am away. As I start to row, I see two otters swimming around in the water in the shadows along the east bank of the river. When they catch sight of me, they quickly disappear.

The sun is not up, but there is enough light to see that it is cloudy with breaks in the lower clouds where the higher clouds are visible. An advantage of fall and winter rowing is the opportunity to experience the changing light of the sunrise. Right now the sky is a blue gray with just enough light to see the waves and swirls in the clouds. As I row up the river, I experience the beginnings of the sun's rise. The lower clouds remain gray, but where I can see through, the higher clouds now appear as islands of orange in that sea of gray.

Just Another Sunrise over the Water

Just past the I-5 bridge, I encounter a number of seagulls sitting on the water together. They seem to regularly collect in the same place during the fall and winter months. At some point, each seagull dips its head and upper body under the water, pulls its head back up, and shakes the water off. They wait until the last minute to get out of my way and fly back to the same place when I have moved on. A little into the row, I see one flock of Canada geese fly in formation across the river from east to west. Not far behind, another flock follows the same route. Happily, Canada geese are not among the hunters' targets. Another advantage of the later sunrise is the opportunity of catching river creatures as they start their day.

The Spencer Island Swamp that runs along part of Steamboat Slough seems to be a favorite for duck hunters. I have been hearing a few gunshots, and I think that my general rule will be to stay in the main river for the rest of the season, particularly on weekends, when there are likely to be more hunters out, or when any degree of fog might hide my presence. I do like Steamboat Slough, where the scenery is more natural. I have never felt in danger during hunting seasons in the past, and my air horn does give me a way to let the hunters know that I am there. I think I will risk it.

The water is calm in the slough, and the evolving colors in the sky are reflecting in the water, distorted only by the waves from my boat and the disturbance created by the stroke of my oars. Not yet visible, the sun has risen to the point where those higher clouds have now turned white. And where it shines through under the cloud cover, there are splashes of orange in the gray. The appearance of the sun is also heating up the air, evaporating the clouds and revealing more and more blue sky.

I have made it to the entrance of Ebey Slough, and since it is Sunday and I have all day, I decide to row up it a ways for a change of scenery. I concentrate on my rowing and am pleased with the speed through the water that I am able to maintain today. Being shorter and wider than *Molly*, *Piper* is slower. However, in comparison to other trips in *Piper* from earlier this year, I am definitely able to maintain a faster speed. Part of it is probably the five pounds I have lost.

There is something swimming ahead of me. I can see it in my forward-view mirror. It sees me, and I hear a slap on the water and see it dive, most certainly a beaver. I've been seeing a number of ripple patterns in the water, and by the time I get there, whatever caused it—beaver, otter, or seal—is gone. I do see the occasional salmon swimming idly at the surface of the water with their dorsal fins exposed. They have been upstream and spawned, and the current has brought them down the river again. With their biological mission completed, they don't seem to care much about what happens to them, and I bump into a number of them as I row. It makes me wonder; with my two sons now grown and gone, maybe I, too, have completed my biological mission. Hopefully, there is some value in older humans for the survival of our species that the salmon doesn't have for its.

I make it to Five-Mile Bend, five miles along the shore from the dock, where my path makes a hard turn to the west, followed in short order with a turn back to the south. That's far enough—time to turn around and head back. The sun is now fully up, and it is still calm. The clouds have largely parted, and the reflection in the water of clouds and sky framed by that of the trees along the bank is inspiring. Every now and again, a very light breeze stirs the water, and the reflection starts to look like an impressionist painting.

As I row back down Ebey Slough, turn south into Steamboat Slough, and head for home, I look at the trees along the river. Some of the deciduous trees still cling to their now-dead leaves, appearing bright orange in the sun's light. Others, stripped of their leaves by the winds and rain of the last few weeks, stand with the complex architecture of their branches against the blue sky. On a high limb of one of these sits an eagle with its head and tail glowing white in the sunlight. It starts to take off and appears to get one of its talons stuck in the branch; it starts to fall upside down, but once loose from the branch, it rights itself in the air and flies back to land again on the tree.

Close to home, I see one lone Canada goose fly over the river behind me. A little later, another follows along. I imagine these guys got a late start on their trip south and are racing to catch up with those flocks I saw leaving earlier. As I reach the dock and lift *Piper* onto my shoulders, a large flock of snow geese flies over high in the sky. They have arrived here from their summer habitat to winter in local fields. There is one large V formation with smaller ones on either side. As they fly along, one of the smaller Vs merges into the main formation. There are so many birds that I have *Piper* on its slings outside the boathouse before they are out of sight. It looks like I was the only rower out today. That's too bad; we may not have another day this nice this year.

~

It has been raining a lot. The TV meteorologist announced that we broke the record for rainfall for the month of October, over a half of foot more than normal, and it didn't slow down much in November or so far in December. Avoiding the rain, and the wind that often come with it has kept me ashore, but I really want to get out. The forecast calls for a bit of a break this weekend, and I really want to get out on the water. Because it is Saturday and I have no place else I have to be all morning, I am going to wait until the sun is fully up to head out. When I arrive at the boathouse, I see the Saturday Masters Rowing Group readying their boats for an outing. It looks like a big group; I think others have felt themselves beached for too long. While I wait my turn, I watch the masters launch two eights and two quads and take off upriver. With the dock now clear, I launch *Piper* and head upriver far behind.

The occasional gunfire reminds me that it's hunting season and I need to stay in the main river. There is a strong current, and the push of the water through the river channel creates a disturbed flow that causes eddies to form. Moving through this water, the boat is pushed this way and that, and I have to row with a little anticipation to keep completely balanced. The river is brown with the dirt washed off the banks upriver, and there are also lots of sticks, branches, and the occasional log that the high water has washed into the river. I am glad I have my forward-view mirror. With its help, I am generally able to see what is washing toward me and get myself to the right or left to avoid trouble. However, I do keep hitting things, pieces of wood so waterlogged and floating so low that I don't see them. Fortunately, what I have been hitting is small, and it just bumps along on the boat, doing no harm.

Passing by the entrance to Steamboat Slough, I see that the clouds to the east have lifted, revealing Three Fingers and Whitehorse Mountains. A little further on, at the Everett river harbor, I see that the cooler water has brought those big seals out of the water to spend some time on the log boom on the east side of the river. Over on the west side, some commercial fishing vessels I hadn't seen for a while have been brought in to spend the winter alongside those here permanently in boat hospice.

Three Fingers and Whitehorse Mountains

Not far past the Highway 2 bridge, I see in my forward-view mirror that one of the masters quads has turned around and is heading my way. I pull far over to the right (my left) to get out of the way. The quad rows by, soon followed by the two eights and the other quad. The synchronized efforts of the rowers generate tremendous power, and the boats move off swiftly.

Now alone on the river, I turn my attention to the surroundings. Except for the blackberry bushes, all of the vegetation along the banks of the river has turned brown. The deciduous trees on both sides of the river have lost all their leaves; their complex branch work stands out sharply against the sky. In the fields to the east, the occasional cow watches me row by; to the west, the homeless camp has grown bigger than it was last winter. When the course of the river permits, I can see the very top of faraway Mount Baker. As I row, it appears to rise up from behind the nearby landscape.

Mount Baker Rises Over the Foreground

The current is strong, and I am rowing much further through the water than I am along the land. Progress is relatively slow, but I make it to the high-voltage power lines crossing the river. Two eagles sit on the top of one of the towers. It is not far from there to the sharp bend in the river at Lowell. The bend sends the water along in a series of eddies, requiring extra control on the oars. Continuing upriver, I hear the whistle blast and see a freight train travel through the Lowell community behind me. From there, it's a half mile along the land to my turnaround at the red farmhouse, but almost a mile through the flowing water.

The return trip downriver is going much quicker. At the end of my travel upriver, the Speed Coach reading of distance through the water was much higher than my GPS reading of distance along the land. Heading downriver, I can see the GPS reading catching up. On some outings, I will end up rowing further along the land than through the water, but that occurs only when the current changes direction or speed while I am out. Today there has been a strong downstream current, and the along-the-land mileage will get closer but will never catch the mileage through the water because I will have spent so much more time rowing slower upriver against the current than I will spend rowing downriver with it.

Not far along, I see a lone eagle in a high branch of one of the trees on the west side of the river. It stands out clearly, showing against the complex network of the tree's branches. I hear its call to me as I row by. Down at water level, three mergansers jump out of the water and fly downriver just above the surface. A little further downriver, a formation of large birds flies over. The high pitch of their honking and their extra-long necks make me think these are swans here for the winter. My guess is confirmed when I see their white wings.

I am feeling strong, rowing a good speed through the water, and aided by the current, I move quickly past Everett's river harbor and into the final stretch to the dock. This will be my last row of the year. Thinking about that reminds me of my last row of the year a couple of years ago. I had just arrived at Eagle Tree; no eagles were present. It was raining, and I had the hood of my jacket over my head, something I have not done since. The hood limited what I could see in my forward-view mirror. I strayed over too close to the shore, and my oar hit an old piling, and over I went. I had capsized a few times before but never that late in the year. The water was cold, but I was close enough to shore that I could stand up and quickly get myself back aboard. From there, I had to row back to the dock in December air temperature. The rowing kept my body core warm, but it was good to get into the shower to bring some heat back into my lower legs and fingers. I am having no such trouble this year.

The current is still running downriver, but a moderate incoming tide has reduced its speed substantially, and the eddies have disappeared. It's cloudy but calm, and the river reflection is silver. As I near the end, a lone seagull flies over to my trail through the water, adjusts its course to mine, flies up over my head and away. Other birds have their seasons, but the seagulls are always here to share the river with me.

It's not long before I am back at the dock, and my rowing for the year is done. Walking up the ramp with *Piper* on my shoulders, I focus, as always, on the large again-leafless alder tree across the road, my Welcoming Tree. I think of the coming and going of its leaves that I observed over the course of the year.

I achieved my goal of rowing over a 1000 miles. Actually, I rowed more miles this year than any year past. Looking ahead, I realize it's time to set that odometer in my head back to zero, and I wonder whether there will be another 1000 miles in me next year. What gives me some confidence are what rowing gives me physically and mentally and what a great place the Snohomish River is in which to do it.

A dedicated rowing enthusiast, Bill Jaquette is out on the water three times a week. His deep connection to rowing has led him to build three boats, join the Everett Rowing Association and Mill Town Rowing, and explore the San Juan Islands in Washington State as well as the Gulf Islands of British Columbia. A follow-up to his first book, *Rowing on the Snohomish*, *Still Rowing on the Snohomish* is a continued tribute to the calming beauty of nature, the joy of rowing, and the passage of time. Bill is also the author of *Gideon's Grandchildren*.

www.ingramcontent.com/pod-product-compliance
Lightning Source LLC
Chambersburg PA
CBHW052144070526
44585CB00017B/1964